The Key to "Revelation"

VOLUME I

The Key to "Revelation"

VOLUME I

Stephen Kaung

CHRISTIAN FELLOWSHIP PUBLISHERS, INC.
NEW YORK

Copyright © 2016

Christian Fellowship Publishers, Inc.
New York
All Rights Reserved.

ISBN: 978-1-68062-991-0

Available from the Publishers at:

11515 Allecingie Parkway
Richmond, Virginia 23235
www.c-f-p.com

Printed in the United States of America

PREFACE

The book of revelation is the last of the sixty-six books of the Bible. As such, it is the concluding word of God and therefore occupies a special position. Whereas a blessing is attached to its reading, a curse is pronounced against anyone adding to its text—thus reflecting how very important is this book of God's word.

The content of this present work, which will be two volumes in length, comprises the text of what were two separate series of messages on Revelation spoken by the author in, respectively, the year 2007 and back during the 1950s. After these many years, and inasmuch as we sense the return of the Lord Jesus to be increasingly imminent, we believe that there is a need to make these spoken words available in print in order that many more of God's people may receive the promised blessing.

The reader will therefore find that this two-volume work when fully published will consist of four Parts. The messages of Part One, The Revelation of Jesus Christ, were delivered (and audio-taped for later possible publication) on 12 to 14 July 2007 at the Western Christian Conference held on the campus of Biola University, Los Angeles, California. The messages comprising the other three Parts—The Testimony of Jesus in Relation to: the Church, the World, and the Jews—were spoken over a lengthy period of time during the decade of the 1950s as a series of weekly Bible studies on the book of Revelation. They were shared by the author before a group of Christians who gathered together in Jamaica, Queens, New York City. It should be noted that the text source for these studies was a series of extensive notes which had been written down by a sister in the Lord who had attended these studies and which had then been transcribed in typewritten form by her as well. It should also be noted that in preparing these transcriptions for today's publication, this entire book's text has been extensively edited, and further, that numerous additional Scripture verses—both texts and/or citations thereof—have been inserted here and there where deemed necessary and/or helpful to the reader.

It is our prayer that all who shall read this book will receive God's blessing in their being better prepared for the imminent return to the earth of our blessed Lord Jesus Christ.

CHRISTIAN FELLOWSHIP PUBLISHERS

Contents—Volume I

Preface 5
Introduction 9

Part One: The Revelation of Jesus Christ

  1—The Church 19
  2—The World 35
  3—The Overcomers 55
  4—The Millennium and Eternity 71

Part Two: The Testimony of Jesus in Relation to the Church

  1—The Testimony of Jesus 91
  2—The Vision of the Son of Man 105
  3—The Meaning of the Vision 123
  4—The Seven Golden Lampstands 137
  5—The Seven Stars 151
  6—The Seven Churches 161
  7—The Man-Child 177
  8—The Man-Child: Firstfruits to God 195
  9—The Kingdom and New Jerusalem 211

Unless otherwise indicated,
Scripture quotations are from the
New Translation by J. N. Darby.

Introduction

Revelation of Jesus Christ, which God gave to him, to shew to his bondmen what must shortly take place; and he signified it, sending by his angel, to his bondman John, who testified the word of God, and the testimony of Jesus Christ, all things that he saw. Blessed is he that reads, and they that hear the words of the prophecy and keep the things written in it; for the time is near.

Revelation 1:1-3

As I waited upon the Lord it seemed as though He wants me to present for us a key to the book of Revelation. Revelation is not only the last book of the Bible but is also the concluding revelation of Jesus Christ. Of course, we know that the whole Bible is the revelation of Jesus Christ.

The Bible is the word of God, and it reveals Jesus Christ. John chapter 5 records Jesus' words: "Ye search the Scriptures, for ye think that in them ye have life eternal, and they it is which bear witness concerning me; and ye will not come to Me" (see vv. 39-40a). And Luke 24 tells us that after the resurrection of the Lord Jesus, He appeared to those two disheartened disciples on their way from Jerusalem to Emmaus. They were disappointed, thinking that everything was lost, and then the Lord had come alongside of them and walked with them. And during that walk Jesus had opened up to them the Scriptures from Moses through the prophets and the Psalms and had explained to them how all these words spoke of Him. Those two disciples had then returned to Jerusalem that same evening to where the apostles were gathered and where the Lord Jesus appeared to all of them and once again explained to them from the Old Testament all the things concerning himself. Hence, from this we know that the entire thirty-nine books of the Old Testament speak of this one subject—the Lord Jesus Christ.

Moreover, in our coming to the New Testament, we know without doubt that the four Gospels therein record the life of the Lord Jesus, and that the book of Acts is the continuation of the speaking and working of Jesus through a mystic, corporate body, the church. Furthermore, all the New Testament epistles explain to us further concerning the Lord Jesus. We can therefore say that the whole Bible constitutes a progressive and continuous revelation of Jesus Christ, with the Bible's last book—Revelation—providing the concluding revelation or the summing up of all the preceding revelations of the previous sixty-five books, thus giving us the full revelation of Jesus Christ.

In fact, the book of Revelation begins with these informative words: "Revelation of Jesus Christ, which God gave to him, to shew to his bondmen what must shortly take place." At its very outset this book tells us that this is the revelation of Jesus Christ, which revelation God gave to His Son, and that in turn His Son showed it to His bondmen. I think this is very clear and unambiguous.

In addition, the apostle Paul has told us in Galatians 1:16 that "it pleased God to reveal his Son in me." From this we conclude that it is always the good pleasure of God the Father to reveal, to speak, or to tell us of His Son, and this last book of the Bible is no exception.

We also learn that this concluding book of the Bible has a special blessing attached to it: "Blessed is he that reads, and they that hear the words of the prophecy and keep the things written in it." So this is a blessed book, and that whoever hears or reads its words of prophecy and keeps them is truly blessed. But in coming to the very end of this book—in its chapter 22—we find that there is also a curse connected with it: that whoever

Introduction

adds anything to, or takes anything from, its words of prophecy will be deprived of all the blessings which have been promised.

Though this is a wonderful, concluding book of the Bible, unfortunately, many of God's people find that this is a most difficult book to understand. Some people even suggest that we not read it at all because it is out of the will of God. That is faulty reasoning because His will is concerned with revealing His beloved Son in the fullest and most complete way, and He wants us to hear that total revelation, to read it, and far more so, He wants us to keep it. And though this is a book of prophecy, and tells us what is going to happen shortly, we must realize that it tells us nothing but what is about the Lord Jesus.

Why is it that today we are so afraid of this last book of the Bible? Why is it that God's people avoid even reading it or studying it? It is because we are confused. Nevertheless, because this is a book that is meant to bless its readers, therefore, Revelation is a book that is supposed to be understood and not create confusion. So, if God wishes to bless its readers, surely He would not give us a sealed book but an open book.

Now this is a book of prophecy telling us what is coming in both the near term and longer term. But if we become bogged down in its many prophetic events, we shall indeed become confused. Some people tell us that all these prophecies are historical in nature. In other words, they believe these have already been fulfilled in the past history of mankind. Other people say, "No, they are partly historical and partly future." If that be true, where will you begin and where will you end? Still other people claim that "all is symbolic; therefore, we must try to discover the explanation for every event and everything which happens—such as the seven seals, the seven trumpets, the seven bowls, etc." Still others declare: "You have to take the whole book literally." But others say in response, "No, it can only be explained symbolically." So because of all these many differences in interpretation, God's people are confused.

The Key to "Revelation"

Now that we are living at the end days, most Christians do seem to be curious about what is going to happen; but as their curiosity increases over time and they begin to touch this highly prophetic book, they find it is impossible to understand.

As was pointed out earlier, this book is the revelation of Jesus Christ which God gave to His Son, and His Son showed to His bondmen, through His bondman the apostle John, all things which are going to happen. But we must recognize the fact that it is clearly stated in its very first verse that "this book is for the purpose of showing to His bondmen what must soon come to pass." Which is to say that if we want to hear it, read it, and keep it, we must each be a bondman of Jesus Christ and that if you and I are not bondmen of Jesus Christ, we will never be able to understand this book because it is not given to us.

In this connection, we will recall that when the Lord was on earth, and because of the hardness of the hearts of the people, He began to speak in parables, thus changing His way of speaking. Instead of speaking plain words to them any longer, Jesus began to use parables: thereafter, whenever He talked to the people He spoke in parables in order that only those who were the Lord's could understand. Whereas the ordinary people merely heard a story, those who were truly the Lord's could understand what was the essential point or points of the story.

Now the same thing is true when it comes to understanding this book of Revelation. Though it is written in the language of signs, visions and wonders, those who are true bondmen of Jesus Christ should have no problem in understanding this remarkable book. Hence, the one essential element in our understanding of this book is that we be bondmen of Jesus Christ.

According to the Scriptures, bondmen are those who love their master and will not leave him and go out free; indeed, as a sign of this commitment they will have their ear pierced, it signifying that their whole life now belongs to the master; and so, they live for one thing only—to serve their master whom

Introduction

they love (Exodus 21:5-6). Accordingly, if we are believers who are saved and redeemed by the precious blood of Jesus, then we all should be bondslaves to *the* master, even the Lord Jesus Christ. We all should be people who are consecrated, who are totally given over to pleasing the Master in all things, and are constrained by the love of Christ (Romans 12:1, II Corinthians 5:14a). We cannot live for ourselves any longer because we no longer belong to ourselves—we belong to Him. We willingly, voluntarily and absolutely surrender our life to Him and live on earth for but one reason: to serve Christ and to serve His purpose. Now if that be our inward attitude, then this concluding book of the Bible should be an open one to us. However, I believe it is important that we discover the key to the entire book of Revelation.

I remember when as a young man, newly saved, that I was very curious about Bible prophecies. I spent much time acquiring books on the Bible's many prophecies and studying them. I even tried to work out a time plan—how things would happen one after another. But the more I studied and the more I read commentaries, the more confused I became. I did not know who to believe or what to conclude about all these prophecies. But thank God, one day He showed me and I realized how very simple it was in understanding Bible prophecies—especially those we find in the Bible's last book.

Granted, in approaching prophetic events, it *can* become quite confusing. We do not know how to explain them or where to place them chronologically. The time factor in the book of Revelation can be very difficult to fathom. How can a timetable be worked out so that this event described in Revelation will happen, and following that, the other event described will occur, or what will next take place and how it will take place. If we study prophecy in that manner, we shall end up being, as it were, lost among the trees. But that is not the way in which God wants us to read, to hear, and to keep what is found in Revelation. Since this is a book whose words need to be kept, how does one keep and obey prophetic events? Many, if not most, of these events lie still in the future, so how are we going to keep them? No one can cause them to come to pass. Nevertheless, we are told that this is a book whose words and events we are to keep, and there is a blessing pronounced upon those who read, hear and keep all things written in it. So one day I came to realize this; that there is a key to this book of Revelation, and that key is quite simple—I saying to myself: "It is simply Jesus Christ himself."

Indeed, Revelation 19:10 clearly spells out for us the key: "the spirit of prophecy is the testimony of Jesus." If we focus upon the *letter* of prophecy we will most certainly become confused. On the other hand, if our focus is upon the *spirit* of prophecy—what this or that prophecy is essentially aiming at— we will not be confused. What, then, are they aiming at? I believe that all these prophecies, all these events, all these future happenings are speaking to us of only one thing—the testimony of Jesus. They all have reference to Jesus and tell us who He is; that is the sum of them all. In fact, in the heart of God there is but one person, His beloved Son Jesus, and it pleases God to reveal His Son to us (cf. Galatians 1:15-16a). And if we are truly His bondmen, then most certainly "the revelation of Jesus Christ"—even this book of Revelation—is meant for us so that we may see Him, know Him, follow Him, and obey Him. But if we do not see Jesus and only see prophetic events, we shall indeed get lost among the trees. So the simplest way through everything prophetic is to return to the simplicity that is in Christ (cf. II Corinthians 11:3b). So what is the spirit of prophecy, the spirit of revelation or vision? It is the testimony of Jesus. The spirit of prophecy testifies to the Lord Jesus Christ.

Now this last book of the Bible actually constitutes the concluding, consummative, and summing up of all the revelations which God has given concerning His Son Jesus Christ in all the preceding Bible books and then bringing it all

Introduction

into fullness to the glory of God. So if we center our attention upon the revelation of Jesus Christ, it will give us new, fresh, and living revelations of Him. Some of these revelations have already been prophesied in the Old Testament, but there are some which are completely new, fresh, and concluding revelations of the Lord. Hence, this is the prayer of my heart, that through this concluding book of the Bible we may come to know Christ in a fuller way, and that knowing Him in such a way, it shall truly stir our hearts and inspire us to worship and give thanks to the Lord.

God willing, therefore, I would like to share on the revelation of Jesus Christ in relation first to the church, which we shall find is covered in Revelation chapters 1-3. In our second session together we will consider the revelation of Jesus Christ in relation to the world, that being covered in chapters 4-19. The third session will focus upon the revelation of Jesus Christ in relation to overcomers, such being covered in chapters 1-19. And finally, our fourth session in this series of messages will be centered upon the revelation of Jesus Christ in relation to the millennium and eternity, such to be found in chapters 20-22. Hopefully, we will cover the essence of this book's entire twenty-two chapters, and I believe we will find that this approach to Revelation is not complicated but very simple. If we all simply adhere to the Person of Jesus Christ, I believe we shall come to know the whole book of Revelation.

Part One
The Revelation of Jesus Christ

Chapter One

The Church

I John, your brother and fellow-partaker in the tribulation and kingdom and patience, in Jesus, was in the island called Patmos, for the word of God, and for the testimony of Jesus. I became in the Spirit on the Lord's day, and I heard behind me a great voice as of a trumpet, saying, What thou seest write in a book, and send to the seven assemblies [or, churches]: to Ephesus, and to Smyrna, and to Pergamos, and to Thyatira, and to Sardis, and to Philadelphia, and to Laodicea.

And I turned back to see the voice which spoke with me; and having turned, I saw seven golden [lampstands], and in the midst of the seven [lampstands] one like the Son of man, clothed with a garment reaching to the feet, and girt about at the breasts with a golden girdle: his head and hair white like white wool, as snow; and his eyes as a flame of fire; and his feet like fine brass, as burning in a furnace; and his voice as the voice of many waters; and having in his right hand seven stars; and out of his mouth a sharp two-edged sword going forth; and his countenance as the sun shines in its power.

And when I saw him I fell at his feet as dead; and he laid his right hand upon me, saying, Fear not; I am the first and the last, and the living one: and I became

The Key to "Revelation"

dead, and behold, I am living to the ages of ages, and have the keys of death and of hades.

Revelation 1:9-18

The apostle John was exiled to the island of Patmos. By this time he was the last of the twelve apostles alive and it is believed that his last ministry had been in Asia Minor. But because of the word of God and of the testimony of Jesus he was exiled to this island. We have been told that he was even ordered to do hard labor, but on one particular Lord's day he had probably been given some free time off duty, and so he was perhaps sitting on a rock looking across the Aegean Sea to Asia Minor. In fact, on a clear day one can see the outline of Asia Minor from Patmos Isle. Without doubt John must have been thinking of the churches to which he had ministered before he was exiled. He was concerned about them because he had been a real shepherd with a true shepherd's heart for God's people. And while he was meditating and thinking about them, suddenly he heard a voice—like the voice of a trumpet—behind him. He looked back and saw a vision, which we today call the Patmos vision. This vision was of seven golden lampstands together with one like the Son of man standing in the midst of them.

The seven golden lampstands are explained to us in Revelation 1:20: "The mystery of the seven stars which thou hast seen on my right hand, and the seven golden [lampstands].—The seven stars are angels of the seven assemblies [or, churches]; and the seven [lampstands] are [those] seven assemblies [or, assemblies]."

These seven golden lampstands represented seven churches in Asia Minor. We know, of course, that at the time of John there were *more* than seven churches or assemblies of God's people in Asia Minor. But the Spirit of God chose seven particular assemblies in a representative way and in a prophetic way out of all the local assemblies there, because during whatever century anyone might be living, all seven features described in this vision to this apostle are reflected in the life of these seven assemblies. Indeed, were we to read church history chronologically we would find that such history began with the declining spiritual situation in the church at Ephesus and descended ultimately to that of the church at Laodicea. So that in coming to the end of this age, the church is actually Laodicean in character. So these seven churches existing at the end of the first century were chosen spiritually as well as prophetically.

"... and in the midst of the seven [lampstands] one like the Son of man ..."

Moreover, we are then told that John saw one like the Son of man standing in the midst of those seven golden lampstands. Let us pause here momentarily to review briefly the earthly life of this Son of man—even the Lord Jesus Christ. In reading the four New Testament Gospels we are shown Jesus' life while He was on earth. Then, in the book of Acts chapter 1 we see Him after He was resurrected and how He appeared to His disciples. Finally, after forty days of various appearances, the resurrected Lord was taken up to heaven. Thus, we are more or less familiar with Jesus in His life on earth because we have the record of the four Gospels and that of Acts 1; but we are not too clear or familiar with the life of the Lord Jesus after He ascended to heaven. What subsequently happened to Him? And what has He been doing there?

We well know that the Old Testament writings had foretold about the coming Messiah. They, as it were, prepared His way for coming to the earth. Then the four Gospels told us how the Word became flesh and tabernacled among men, He having been full of grace and truth (John 1:14). Such was His relatively short life on earth. But after He ascended back to heaven, what has been going on since then? What has He been doing there?

The Key to "Revelation"

This we learn from the concluding revelation that is given in the very last book of the Bible. That is why this book now before us is so important, because it sums up, concludes, and fills to the fullest the revelation of Jesus Christ.

So we have in the Patmos vision one like the Son of man standing in the midst of the seven golden lampstands, which thus is an intimation to us of exactly what—after Jesus' ascension back to heaven—He has been doing there. For I am reminded of what the book of Hebrews has told us, in summing up in just a few short words what Jesus had been doing while He was on earth and what He has been doing ever since up in heaven: "... Jesus the apostle and high priest whom we confess" (see 3:1b). With regard to His earthly work Jesus is the Apostle, the Sent One of God, the Anointed of God, who was sent to accomplish a mission. In fact, Jesus was always saying, "I was sent" (see, e.g., Matthew 15:24; John 3:17a, 34a; 6:38; 20:21). He was continually acknowledging that He had been sent on a mission by His Father. Jesus, therefore, is *the* Apostle, who has accomplished an impossible mission. And upon His having fulfilled that mission, Jesus declared just before His death: "It is finished—it is accomplished" (see John 19:30).

But then, having been buried, Jesus arose from the dead and ascended back to His Father in heaven. The question therefore naturally arises: What has He been doing there? Well, because His earthly work is now finished, let us not conclude from that that Jesus is now sitting in heaven dozing off and simply waiting for all His enemies to become His footstool (cf. Hebrews 10:13). Not in the least. On the contrary, the Lord Jesus is there in heaven working harder than any one of us and all of us put together, for Hebrews also tells us that He intercedes for us incessantly, without ceasing (7:25b). The risen and ascended Lord Jesus continues working for us in completing still further what He had finished doing while He was on earth but now in that second capacity of His which is cited in Hebrews 3:1: *the* High Priest of God. And hence, the ministry of the Lord Jesus in heaven is as the royal High Priest, and that is the scene of His labor on our behalf which we find in the Patmos vision: there was one like the Son of man standing in the midst of the seven golden lampstands.

It is extremely important that we not be ignorant of the ministry of the Lord Jesus in heaven. Indeed, it is just as important as was His ministry on earth because whereas His ministry on earth laid the foundation, His ministry in heaven completes the work that God has been after ever since the Fall of mankind. Let us thank and praise God, that Jesus as the Apostle did indeed become our Redeemer: He sacrificed himself for us and saved us. But can we live a Christian life after we are saved without knowing of, and benefiting from, His ministry in heaven? Impossible! That is the reason there is so much failure and weakness among God's people. We were saved by most certainly leaning upon the Lord Jesus *alone*, but after we are saved too many of us try to live our Christian life by leaning upon ourselves alone. We no longer depend upon Him because we think all of His work for us is finished. Not so, for He is not finished laboring for us yet. Rather, it is just the beginning. Jesus is there as our royal High Priest interceding for us without ceasing, and whoever will come to God through Him, He can and *will* save that one to the uttermost, that is to say, completely (Hebrews 7:25a). If we want to be saved completely, we must depend solely upon our High Priest. Thank God, we do have a holy High Priest, who is also a royal High Priest after the order of Melchisedec, ever living for us and ministering to us today (Hebrews 6:20b, 7:24). And such is the very work of the Lord Jesus today in heaven: He is *applying* to us what He had accomplished on earth in having redeemed us.

From the book of Hebrews, which we have cited several times already, we may deduce the idea that Jesus is the High Priest who is able to sympathize with us, intercede for us, and save us to the uttermost *individually* and, probably neglect what this same ministry of His is today to the *church*. We too often think of His ministry as High Priest in terms of it being solely for the individual believer. We praise God that that aspect of His ministry is quite true, but for a long, long time I failed to see the ministry of the Lord Jesus in heaven as being for the church as a whole. Yet even in this same book of Hebrews we are told that we have a holy High Priest who has sat down at the right hand of the throne of the Majesty in the heavens and is ministering to the true tabernacle established by God (8:1). This confirms that the Lord Jesus ministers in heaven not only to individual believers but also to the church as a whole. And this is the dramatic scene which we find being played out in Revelation chapters 1-3, which is the very ministry of the Lord Jesus to the churches of this age in His capacity as the royal High Priest.

One element which we need to take special notice of here is that in the Patmos vision John saw seven golden lampstands and then he saw one like the Son of man standing in the midst of them. So that as we contemplate this vision we see that the seven lampstands serve as a background but in the *foreground* there is one like the Son of man. I think this is very important for us to lay hold of because we cannot emphasize the church more than we do of Christ. The church is for Christ and not solely that Christ is for the church. Christ is always in the foreground, but He is always being seen against the background of the church. Otherwise, you will not see Him. How can the world see Christ if it is not through the church—the golden lampstand? Let us recall that there were only two pieces of furniture in the ancient tabernacle that were made wholly of gold—the mercy seat was one and the other was the lampstand (Exodus 25:17-18, 31). Is that not wonderful! Whereas the mercy seat speaks of Christ, whose nature is symbolized by gold—and nothing but gold, the lampstand speaks of the church, and the church too should be symbolized by gold and not wood—only gold. Wood in Scripture represents man but gold represents the divine nature.

The Church

What is the church? The church is Christ coming to the world in a corporate expression—the church being nothing *but* Christ. If we add anything of ourselves into the church we spoil it; we corrupt it. And further, a lampstand is only a means to an end; it is not the end itself. Today, of course, people display lampstands as a decorative end in itself; yet the lampstand, were it able to speak, would be crying out, "This is not what I am made for! I am here solely to uplift the light that the world may see." That, in fact, is what the church is to be: the church is never to speak of itself or draw attention to itself; instead, it speaks of Christ and lifts Him up for all the world to see. He is the light and the church is only a lampstand.

In the Patmos vision John saw this person and described him as "one like the Son of man." John knew the Son of man rather well for had he not often lain upon Jesus' breast? (John 13:25, 21:20) Yet John said here, "like the Son of man." There is some difference to be noted here. He knew Jesus as the Son of man on earth quite intimately, but when he beheld that Man in the vision, it was indisputably Jesus, yet He was different—*like* the Son of man. What accounted for this difference? It was because Jesus was now in glory. When He was on earth, He was in His humiliation, but now He is in His glory. He is the same Person but with a difference. Even so, John knew it was the Lord, the royal High Priest.

"... I saw seven golden [lampstands], and in the midst of the seven [lampstands] one like the Son of man, clothed with a garment reaching to the feet ... "

He was clothed with a robe that went down to His feet. That is the robe of a priest and speaks of Him as being full of righteousness.

"... and girt about at the breasts with a golden girdle ... "

When you wear a long robe, you must gird it up around your waist if you want to work; but here we are told that the golden girdle was worn about His breast because the work of redemption is over and done with and now it is the labor of love in which the Lord Jesus is engaged. He is full of love.

"... his head and hair white like white wool, as snow ... "

This Son of man's head and hair were white as snow, like white wool—which bespeaks of Him as being full of wisdom.

"... and his eyes as a flame of fire ... "

Also, His eyes were as a flame of fire and full of light—that which is able to penetrate into another's very being.

"... and his feet like fine brass, as burning in a furnace ... "

He also had feet like fine brass as though it were burning in a furnace—signifying the fact of His being full of judgment. Brass—such as was found in the tabernacle's brazen altar—always speaks of judgment.

"... and his voice as the voice of many waters ... "

Then, too, His voice was as the voice of many waters—He is full of majesty, for how majestic is the sound of many waters!

"... and having in his right hand seven stars ... "

Furthermore, He had in His right hand seven stars—such betokening that He is full of responsibility and faithfulness.

"... and out of his mouth a sharp two-edged sword going forth ..."

Moreover, out of His mouth a sharp two-edged sword was going forth—bespeaking the fact that this Man is full of power, a power that can even penetrate and divide man's soul and spirit (Hebrews 4:12a).

"... and his countenance as the sun shines in its power"

Finally, John saw that this Son of man's countenance was as the sun shining in its power—an indication that this Man is full of inner beauty.

That, then, was the ten-fold description of the Son of man. He is our royal High Priest who is after the order of Melchisedec. Melchisedec was a priest but he was also a king—a king of righteousness and peace (Hebrews ch. 7). So, too, this is our High Priest today.

"And when I saw him I fell at his feet as dead; and he laid his right hand upon me, saying, Fear not; I am the first and the last, and the living one: and I became dead, and behold, I am living to the ages of ages, and have the keys of death and of hades."

John did not feel threatened by the sight of the seven golden lampstands, but when he saw *the Son of man*, he fell down as one dead. It was too much for him. Whenever we see the glory of the Lord—even the glory of the Lord as the royal High Priest—we, too, will fall down as dead. All *our* beauty—whatever glory *we* may have attained—will turn into corruption and ash. How can anyone stand before such glory that is the Lord's?

When you contemplate the Lord Jesus as the High Priest, what will be your understanding? What will be your feeling towards Him? You will probably feel that He is merciful, sympathetic, tender, meek, and lowly because that is what you know of Him in His earthly life. But you may never contemplate Jesus in heaven as still being that meek and lowly Lamb; yet there is a royal glory in Him and about Him that is overwhelming. You cannot treat Him any way you like. There will come over you a holy fear. When you behold the glory of the Lord in His being the royal High Priest for you and for the church, there will come over you an immense sense of awe because you know you yourself do not come close at all to measuring up: He is so holy and we are so sinful. What we deem our beauty to be will turn immediately into ashes. For, by comparison, that is what it is. The beloved John fell down as one dead. He could see instantly the failure of his ministry but he could also see his own moral and spiritual failure. He did not measure up in the least to what the royal High Priest will offer. The possibilities are there but we—like John—cannot but sense a huge personal failure.

We need to see the glory of the Son of man. We need to see Him at the right hand of the Father. We need to see Him as the royal High Priest. And in doing so, that will instantly reduce us and truly put us into the state of death. But thank God, the merciful and gracious High Priest laid His hand upon John and said: "Fear not, I am the first and the last and the living One. Behold, I died, but I am living forevermore, and I hold in *my* hands the keys of death and Hades." By this tender action and by these words the Lord Jesus was comforting John: "It is true; even you have not yet measured up to the standard. I am the standard. I have accomplished all things. And now I offer it to you and it is all yours, but you have not really apprehended all that I have apprehended you for. That is true, but I am going to do it. You cannot do it, that is certain, but I can. The church has failed but I will never fail."

The Church

"Write therefore what thou hast seen ..." (1:19a)

Then He told John to write to the seven churches in Asia. We know that these seven cited churches in Asia Minor were still in existence towards the end of the first century. The Lord Jesus had committed His testimony to the church. Let me put it this way: While He was on earth, and in view of the cross, He had told Peter and His other disciples, "You are Peter; on this rock I will build My church, and the gates of Hades shall not prevail against it" (see Matthew 16:18). He said, "I will build My church on this rock." When did He begin to build? He began to build after He had ascended on high and the Holy Spirit had come down on the day of Pentecost. On that day the 120 believers, who were gathered together in one spirit and praying for ten days, were baptized into one body. That was the beginning of the church on earth. And although while on earth Jesus had indeed laid the foundation of the building of the church, He really began to build after His resurrection and His ascension back to heaven. Therefore, what He is doing there is building His church. No one can build the church except the Lord Jesus, and He is building it from heaven in His position as the royal High Priest.

What is involved in building the church? What exactly is real building? The real act of building is that first He builds himself into each one of us, then He eliminates us and puts all that He is into us together. That is actually what the building of the church is. I used to employ a formula with which our brother T. Austin-Sparks was not happy. When I first employed that formula, I had apologized to brother Sparks and said that I would only employ it temporarily because I realize one cannot put spiritual things into a formula. That formula went something like the following.

Suppose there are only three Christians on earth, and these three Christians are the best ones. Who do you think they would be? I would say, John, Peter, and Paul. What is the church? Is it John plus Peter plus Paul equals the church? Of course, we know it is not. Is it the Christ in John, plus the Christ in Peter, plus the Christ in Paul equals the church? Yes and no. It is indeed the Christ in John but it is also minus John, it is indeed plus the Christ in Peter but also minus Peter, and it is indeed plus the Christ in Paul but also minus Paul—and *that* equals the church. This, in fact, is what I Corinthians 12:12 declares: "So also is the Christ."

What is the building of the church? It is the process of Christ building himself into us and then He builds what He is in us all together. That is why nobody can do that except the Lord himself. So He is engaged in heaven in building the church, and the way He does it is to commit himself to the church. He reveals himself to the church. But let us realize that every revelation of His is a commitment and with the commitment there is a responsibility. Hence, when God reveals His Son in us (cf. again Galatians 1:15-16a), He commits His Son to us, and that is our testimony. That is how we live, and that is how we show to the world what we are. So in this Patmos vision we find the Lord is in heaven as the royal High Priest, and He is ministering to the true tabernacle not made with man's hands. And that is the church.

The Lord is ministering today to the church, and that is what we find Him doing in the vision which John saw. The risen, ascended Christ is walking among the seven golden lampstands as the High Priest, observing whether or not the light is shining. He has committed His revelation, His testimony, even himself to the church, and He is looking for himself there. How much of himself can He find in the church? How much has been lost that has been revealed? How faithful are we in responding in fullness to what He has revealed of himself to us? In fact, what is the state of our testimony? Is the light burning or smoking or fading? If the Lord finds that there is something scorched or dying out, He will use the golden snuffer to apply discipline upon us in order to bring us back to freshness and livingness in Him by trimming off, as it were, the

The Church

scorched wick, and then He will pour fresh oil of the Spirit into it so that it will again burst into flame and produce light once more. Now that is what the Lord has been doing on high from the day He ascended even to this present hour, and that is the true building of the church. And hopefully we have an ear to hear what the Spirit is saying to the churches: "he that overcomes." Now that is what the Lord is looking for.

Yet, what do we actually see in the church today? If we look into ourselves or look about at the assemblies of God throughout the whole earth, probably we will be very disappointed or become highly discouraged. We may even conclude that the church as a glorious church without spot or wrinkle or any other blemish and suitable for the Bridegroom—who is the Lord Jesus—is something impossible ever to attain. In this connection, you have probably previously heard that once on one occasion brother Sparks asked brother Watchman Nee: "What do you think is the hardest prophecy in the Bible to be fulfilled?" And brother Nee replied, "What we find in Ephesians 5—a glorious church without spot or wrinkle or any of such sort, fit for the Lord Jesus the Bridegroom." Indeed, humanly speaking, this will be the most difficult prophecy to be fulfilled. But thank God, after Jesus finished His work on earth, He began building His church on that foundation and is still building His church, making her a glorious church just as He himself is glorious, being without any spot or wrinkle or any other stain. Yes, humanly, this seems impossible, yet nothing is impossible with God (Matthew 19:26, Mark 10:27). What the Lord Jesus is doing in heaven is building up His church in order that she may be a total reflection of himself devoid of any shade, shadow, or distortion of any kind—just as He is. If the Lord Jesus is going to do it, He will most certainly do it.

Be all that as it may, nevertheless, whenever I myself contemplate the situation of the church today, I sense a feeling of hopelessness and I become very depressed. How can the church ever become a glorious church without spot or wrinkle or any other blemish, suitable for Christ the Bridegroom (cf. Ephesians 5:25-27)? Impossible! The more I muse upon the matter, the more I look around, and the more the years pass by, it seems as though the state of the church is fading, ever fading, even on the verge of fading totally away. But, then, when I read again in the first three chapters of this book of Revelation, suddenly, it dawns upon me that I have forgotten the royal High Priest and His unfailing ministry. I may fail, and I do fail. We may fail, and we will fail. But He can *never* fail. He is ever working. He is constantly walking among the seven golden lampstands looking for himself, and He calls us to repent. Our faithful High Priest uses the golden snuffer, disciplining us, pouring again and again more oil into the lamp that is the church.

Yet how do we know that the constancy of the unfailing ministry of the risen, ascended Lord Jesus will achieve, in the end, the intended goal? The answer is to be found in the final two chapters, 21-22, of Revelation. There we behold a giant golden lampstand—the new Jerusalem—and everything in it speaks of Christ. The glory of that city is the glory of God. And thus we know that the goal will be achieved, that the most difficult of all Biblical prophecies to be fulfilled *will* be fulfilled. Admittedly, if we seek to visualize its accomplishment today with our naked eyes, we shall not see it, for we today cannot find any perfect church. As someone has wisely observed, "If, in fact, there is on earth a perfect church, then were you or I to join her, she would instantly become imperfect." No, instead, we are to visualize the matter with the eyes of faith. Let us not look at environment or at appearance, but let us look off to Jesus; for the more we look away to Him— the great royal High Priest who is ministering to His church— the more we will believe and the more hopeful we will become, now realizing that all *will* be done. In fact, one day we shall all be rejoicing in that new Jerusalem—the glorious church now entirely fitting for the Bridegroom, our Lord Jesus. For the light is God, and the lamp is the Lamb (Revelation 21:23). And hence, the deed is done! And it is most glorious!

Now because of all this, I feel comforted, and I feel hopeful once more. If we only look at ourselves, we will surely give up and declare: Hopeless! But if we look away to Jesus—fixing our eyes upon Him who is the Key and the Author and Finisher of faith (Hebrews 12:2a)—we can lift up our heads and give thanks to God.

May the Lord bless us all.

Chapter Two

The World

And I saw on the right hand of him that sat upon the throne a book, written within and on the back, sealed with seven seals. And I saw a strong angel proclaiming with a loud voice, Who is worthy to open the book, and to break its seals? And no one was able in the heaven, or upon the earth, or underneath the earth, to open the book, or to regard [or, look into] it. And I wept much because no one had been found worthy to open the book nor to regard it. And one of the elders says to me, Do not weep. Behold, the lion which is of the tribe of Juda, the root of David, has overcome so as to open the book, and its seven seals.

And I saw in the midst of the throne and of the four living creatures, and in the midst of the elders, a Lamb standing, as slain, having seven horns and seven eyes, which are the seven Spirits of God which are sent into all the earth: and it came and took it out of the right hand of him that sat upon the throne. And when it took the book, the four living creatures and the twenty-four elders fell before the Lamb, having each a harp and golden bowls full of incenses, which are the prayers of the saints. And they sing a new song, saying, Thou art worthy to take the book, and to open its seals; because thou hast been slain, and hast redeemed to God, by thy blood, out of every tribe, and tongue, and people, and nation, and made them

The Key to "Revelation"

to our God kings and priests; and they shall reign over the earth.

And I saw, and I heard the voice of many angels around the throne and the living creatures and the elders; and their number was ten thousands of ten thousands and thousands of thousands; saying with a loud voice, Worthy is the Lamb that has been slain, to receive power, and riches, and wisdom, and strength, and honour, and glory, and blessing. And every creature which is in the heaven and upon the earth and under the earth, and those that are upon the sea, and all things in them, heard I saying, To him that sits upon the throne, and to the Lamb, blessing, and honour, and glory, and might, to the ages of ages. And the four living creatures said, Amen; and the elders fell down and did homage.

Revelation 5:1-14

And the seventh angel sounded his trumpet: and there were great voices in the heaven, saying, The kingdom of the world of our Lord and of his Christ is come, and he shall reign to the ages of ages. And the twenty-four elders, who sit on their thrones before God, fell upon their faces, and worshipped God, saying, We give thee thanks, Lord God Almighty, He who is, and who was, that thou hast taken thy great power and hast reigned.

Revelation 11:15-17

We are considering before the Lord this matter of a key to Revelation. And as I indicated yesterday, I believe the reason many of God's people are confused about this book of the Bible is because they become bogged down in the various prophetic events leading up to, and including, Jesus' return to the earth in kingdom glory. Yet the Lord had himself told His disciples that nobody knows the date of His return—only the Father. Sad to say, however, in church history there have been many people who have told the world that on a certain day the Lord would come back; but of course, the various dates they had suggested came and went with nothing of the sort happening.

It is true that this is a book of prophecy, but I believe that God reveals to us its words of prophecy not for the purpose that we might become prophets but for an entirely different reason. For as was pointed out last time, it is said in Revelation 19:10 that "the spirit of prophecy is the testimony of Jesus"; the inference from which is that God is not interested in prophetic events *per se* but in His beloved Son, and that through the words of prophecy in this book He is wishing to reveal to its readers Jesus Christ in the fullest way. Therefore, this book is itself called "The Revelation of Jesus Christ," and it is a revelation of Him given to His bondmen. So may we truly appreciate this book, and through it see, by the grace of God, a full revelation of the Lord Jesus.

We began with a revelation of Jesus Christ in relation to the church, and as we saw last time this is recorded for us in the first three chapters of Revelation. When Jesus was on earth as the Apostle or Sent One of God, He accomplished a mission that, humanly speaking, is impossible. Yet, having been crucified on the cross, He declared, "It is finished." And thus the work of redemption was accomplished on earth, and hence Jesus, as it were, laid the foundation of the church while He was on earth. Then He ascended back to heaven, and there—in His position as the royal High Priest—He is building His church: He is ministering in and to the true tabernacle not made by man. The church is the golden lampstand, and the responsibility of the church is to uplift Christ. So in the Patmos vision which John beheld we see the Lord Jesus as the royal High Priest walking among the seven churches looking for himself and thus determining whether the light is burning and His testimony is shining. And if He sees something missing, He will minister to the church by either taking away the scorched wick or pouring fresh oil of the Spirit into it so that the light will burn once more. That, then, is the ministry of the Lord Jesus in heaven, which is the scene that is presented in Revelation's first three chapters.

Now the next facet I wish for us to consider together is the revelation of Jesus Christ in relation to the world, which is unveiled for us in Revelation chapters 4-19. In this section we see the Lamb on the throne. We are familiar with the Lord Jesus as the Lamb of God because the Gospel of John unveils this to us. We all know that of the four New Testament Gospels John is the only one which not only records the life of the Lord Jesus but also actually explains the meaning of Christ. In fact, that is the reason it opens with these words of explanation: "In the beginning was the Word, and the Word was with God, and the Word was God. ... The Word became flesh and tabernacled among men, full of grace and truth" (see John 1:1, 14a, c).

After Jesus was baptized He was led by the Spirit of God into the wilderness. There He was tempted by the devil forty days and nights, and He overcame the enemy. Following that is when John the Baptizer saw Him, and when he did so he declared: "Behold the Lamb of God who takes away the sin of the world" (John 1:29). The next day John was with two of his disciples when Jesus was passing by, and he again cried out: "Behold, the Lamb of God" (v. 35). And the two disciples of John left him and followed Jesus. Hence, it can be said that when Jesus was on earth, He was the Lamb of God.

When did the Lord Jesus begin to be the Lamb of God? Was it after His incarnation? I Peter informs us of this: "Knowing that you have been redeemed, not by corruptible things, as silver or gold, from your vain manner of life handed down to you from your fathers, but by precious blood, as of a lamb without blemish and without spot, the blood of Christ,

The World

foreknown indeed before the creation of the world, but who has been manifested at the end of times for your sakes" (see 1:18-20). Peter declares that even before the foundation of the world Jesus was foreknown by God as the Lamb.

In order for us to better understand what had taken place in the past, let us employ here a few human expressions. At the commencement of all beginnings, there was God, the Supreme One. And with God there was the Word—that is to say, there was His expression, His image, His speech, His *Logos*—even as the Gospel of John has declared: "In the beginning was the Word (Greek: *Logos*), and the Word was with God, and the Word was God."

Back then in ages past there was such a wonderful, unparalleled fellowship between God as Father and the Word as Son, because it all occurred in the Holy Spirit. It was all of everlasting life and full of light, righteousness, and love. The Father and the Son shared everything with each other and did so equally: indeed, they kept nothing back the one from the other. Briefly stated, they were perfectly one.

Let us imagine that when they were together in the Spirit they must have had such wholesome conversation, they expressing themselves to one another unhinderedly. For example, the Father might have said to the Son on one occasion: "How I love You. And in view of that, I want to express My love to You in concrete fashion. [Does not love always seek to find expression?] How, then, can I express My love towards You, My Son? I know what I shall do—I shall create the world and all things in it and give all to You." "Beyond all that," continued the Father, "because You are love just as I am, such love which You yourself will express must have some response too. For even with the material, physical world that I will create and give to You, it will not satisfy You. Such a gift cannot express My love to You fully, so I shall want to create a being in Our image and after Our likeness, with the hope and intention that this creature which I will create will be able to respond to

Your love, may understand Your love, may receive Your love, and even return love to You so as to satisfy Your heart. That is what I very much want to do for You."

But being the Omniscient One, He who knows the end from the beginning may have further said to the Son: "Nevertheless, it is certain that I will be confronted with a problem because I can foresee that what I shall have created for You will cause there to arise a rebellion—yet not only among the angelic hosts of heaven but even also among all of mankind on earth who will be created in Our image. Now, then, My Son, what can be done to resolve this problem?" And the Son may have stepped forward, saying: "Father, proceed with Your desire; for if this is Your will, I am willing to offer Myself as a sacrificial lamb, so that Your will may be accomplished." So, possibly a conversation such as this, held in eternity past among the triune Godhead in perfect fellowship one with another, may account for how, even before the creation of the world, God the Son already became a lamb—even the Lamb of God.

A further intimation of this can be found in chapter 13 of Revelation: "... all whose names had not been written in the book of life of [or, belonging to] the Lamb that was slain from the founding of the world" (v. 8b). Here we find mentioned not only the Lamb but the slain Lamb. The book of life belongs to the Lamb slain, and the Lamb was slain from the foundation or creation of the world. As was noted earlier, I Peter reads: "... a lamb ..., foreknown *before* the foundation of the world" (1:19b-20a). From even before the foundation of the world He is the Lamb. As soon as the world began God the Son was already the slain Lamb. "The Lamb" speaks of the eternal purpose of God and the will of God, and "the slain Lamb" betokens His work of redemption. Perhaps there is no difference between "*before* the foundation of the world" and "*from* the foundation of the world," since some New Testament scholars tell us that the Greek preposition employed in both passages can be translated either *before* or *from*. And if that be the case, it is a distinction without a significant difference, since the Lord Jesus had become the Lamb of God *already* slain before and from the creation of the world.

In Ephesians 1 we are told that we believers in Jesus have been chosen even before the foundation of the world. On what basis have we been chosen? Such choosing is based upon the fact that the Lord Jesus is the Lamb slain from the foundation of the world. And hence, that is our eternal security, for which we must thank God. Just think of the love of God expressed towards us: Can any of us imagine this?!? It is beyond our comprehension, yet this is the character of our Father-God and this is the character of our Lord Jesus. Indeed, this is the revelation of Jesus as the Lamb slain from the foundation of the world, and it is related to our having been chosen. In the fullness of time, however, the Word became flesh and tabernacled among humanity on the earth as one of us. And during His days on earth as a man, He was a lamb—even the sacrificial Lamb of God.

Now immediately after the first man sinned, God clothed that naked man with animal skins. From this we can correctly conclude that because man sinned, an innocent animal—most likely a lamb—had to be slain for his sake, yet not only for the blood that was required to redeem him from his sin but that he might be clothed. And throughout these many centuries, even well before the first Passover, those who feared God were wont to offer up sacrifices. Numerous innocent animals were killed and much blood had to be shed because such is the way of salvation. And then on the day of that first Jewish Passover every household of the Israelites had to prepare a lamb, spotless and pure. Then the lamb was killed, the blood was shed, and then placed upon each home's doorposts and lintel, so that the angel of destruction—seeing the sprinkled blood—would pass over that house: a physical picture of God's redemption (Exodus 12:21ff.).

Year after year thereafter, hundreds, thousands, even numberless lambs were slain; yet, as we are told by the writer of the New Testament book of Hebrews, the blood of lambs and goats cannot really redeem us from our sins (cf. 10:4, 11). These served as types and symbols, until one day John the Baptizer declared: "Behold the Lamb of God who takes away the sin of the world!" Finally, God's Lamb—Jesus the Christ—had come, and throughout His entire earthly life He lived a lamb-life. He came to His own people because the world's humanity had been created by Him, but His own received Him not (John 1:11). He came into this world as the Lamb-King. Yes, indeed, He came as a king, but as a king who was lamb-like in every way. Or to phrase it another way: He came in lowliness and meekness.

This Lamb-King's coming was prophesied in the Old Testament book of Zechariah: "Behold, your King cometh sitting on a colt of an ass, meek and lowly" (see 9:9). Jesus as the Lamb-King sought to bring His heavenly kingdom into the world, but how different that is from the kingdom of this world. For did He not say to the Roman Governor of Israel, Pontius Pilate: "My kingdom is not of this world; for the way of My kingdom is completely different: it is marked by meekness and lowliness, humility, and serving and sacrificing" (cf. John 18:33-37). But the world rejected Jesus, and so He was crucified.

Jesus was crucified as the Lamb of God and by means of His crucifixion He completed the work of redemption. His blood was shed for the remission of our sins, and His body was broken to give life to us in order that we might be joined to God in Christ Jesus. It was a huge victory, thus moving the Lord to declare with finality: "It is finished!" (see John 19:30)

Now quite naturally we are concerned about what happened *to us* when the Lamb of God was slain on the cross. It is true, of course, that man is at the center of Jesus' work of redemption, mankind being the apple of God's eye; but we need to understand that with the fall of man there came in also the fall of the world. As a matter of fact, the entire world entered into corruption and vanity, it having fallen into the hands of Satan, the enemy of God. Indeed, he became the god and prince of this world, having organized it to oppose the true God. And though we are prone to think only of ourselves and our redemption, we must come to the realization that when Jesus was crucified on the cross, He accomplished far more than simply redeeming us from our sins, as great and wonderful as that is. He additionally accomplished that which would ensure the recovery of the world back to God. Having—like mankind—fallen into vanity and corruption itself, this world shall be restored and all things therein shall be brought back to the feet of the Son's beloved Father.

It is of interest to note that well into Jesus' earthly ministry He was heard to say the following: "The time has now come for judgment upon the world, and the prince of this world will be driven out" (see John 12:31). In the world which God had created for His Son there had indeed arisen the expected rebellion, and so, He created man for the purpose, among other reasons, of using him to resolve the problem of subduing and bringing back all things to himself, but man also committed the sin of rebellion. Therefore, the Son of God came forth as a man—a man after God's heart. And as a man the Son overcame the prince of this world. For when He was lifted up on the cross, the prince of this world was cast out (cf. John 12:31). There on Calvary's cross the Lord Jesus fought the most critical battle of the universe and won decisively. And in doing so He took the world away from the enemy, and on the basis of that victory the Lord Jesus began to reconcile all things in heaven and on earth back to the fullness and glory of God.

The apostle Paul, in his Letter to the Colossians, explained the matter this way: "Having led principalities and authorities as His captives, He made a spectacle of them publicly, overcoming them by the cross" (see 2:15). Hence, what the Lord Jesus accomplished on the cross was much, much more than simply redeeming us human beings: it also included laying the foundation for the recovering of the world and all the things He had created in it back to God. For Paul has further explained this matter in this same letter with these words: "God was pleased to reconcile by His Son all things to the fullness of God himself, having made peace by the blood of His cross—all things reconciled by Him, whether they be things on the earth or things in the heavens" (see 1:19-20).

Oh how we need to see that wider horizon and not only think of ourselves in relation to the cross of Jesus. We need to understand that when Jesus was crucified on the cross, the world too was crucified (cf. Galatians 6:14b), this world's prince was driven out, and all things therein were reconciled back to God. The enmity of all things against God was taken away (Ephesians 2:16), and all things upon earth and in the heavens shall ultimately be reconciled back to the fullness of God by the blood of Christ's cross (Colossians 1:19-20). Christ Jesus will reconcile all things and bring them back in His fullness to the feet of His Father. That is why Scripture tells us that after the Lord Jesus arose from the dead, the Father said to Him, "Sit at My right hand until I make all Your enemies Your footstool" (see Psalm 110:1, Hebrews 10:12-13).

This leads us to the scene pictured for us in Revelation 5; but to understand it more clearly and fully we probably need to review the content of chapter 4 immediately preceding, because there we learn that a door was opened for John into heaven and a voice said to him: "Come up here and I will show you the things which must take place after this." So John was immediately found in the Spirit and was taken up to heaven. There John saw a vision of the glory of the Creator. Chapter 4 provides a marvelous replay of the glory of creation because John beheld and heard praise and worship constantly being offered up to One who, seated on a throne there, had created all things, and for His will they had been created and have their being. For John, it was none other than a vision of the glory of both the Creator and His creation.

If, for the apostle John, chapter 4 served as a vision of the glory of creation, then chapter 5 provided him with a vision of the glory of redemption. It too is a replay—but a replay of what must have been the culmination of the ascension back to heaven of the risen Lord Jesus. We will recall that when He ascended up to heaven, the disciples were looking upward and saw the Lord Jesus ascending; but then a cloud hid Him from their sight. They could not see Him anymore, but as they continued looking up, two men dressed in white appeared and said, "Men of Galilee, why are you standing here looking up into the sky? This Jesus who is taken up from you into heaven will return in like manner as you have witnessed Him going into heaven" (see Acts 1:9-11). Probably, some people like the doubting apostle Thomas might assert: "Did the Lord Jesus actually reach heaven and the throne? Perhaps He was cast down somewhere. Where is the proof of His having reached the heavenly throne of God?" Well, the proof that He arrived there is the vision of Revelation 5 which John saw, for it provides us with the concluding phase of Jesus' ascending from earth to heaven. How, though, do we know that the context of Revelation 5 is indeed a replay of the culminating scene of the arrival at God's heavenly throne *of the risen Lord Jesus*? Well, the One who appears there is a Lamb, and a Lamb who looks as though it had been slain (in fact, the original Greek is to be most accurately translated as, *newly slain*); and furthermore, the Lamb is standing in the very center of the throne and encircled by the twenty-four elders and the four living creatures—all elements as were exactly depicted in the throne vision of Revelation 4.

On Calvary's cross the Lord Jesus was slain as *the* sacrificial Lamb, but in Revelation 5 the Lamb is resurrected because it is standing—though newly slain. So what we see depicted in Revelation 5 is believed to be a replay of the concluding phase of the risen Lord's ascension. And when He ascended on high, He received the nations, the world, and all things in it as His inheritance, and this is what is portrayed in Revelation 5 as having happened after the Lord's arrival at the throne. The One who sits upon the throne is God, the Creator of all things. And in His hand there is a book or a scroll, but it is sealed. And there came forth a voice by a strong angel that could be heard in heaven, upon earth, and even underneath the earth. And the voice inquired, "Who is worthy to take the book and open its seals?" The challenge thus went out, but there was no response—no response in heaven, nor on earth, nor under the earth. In other words, neither angels, nor man, nor devils and demons—no one—was worthy to take the book and open it. And what occurred next is that the beloved disciple John wept much.

Now we may wonder why he should have wept and wept. He went on weeping profusely because he understood that this book is the title deed to the world—to the entire creation. God is the Creator and He holds the title deed to everything which has been created. He is the Owner of the world and all things in it. We will recall from the Old Testament book of Genesis that God had commissioned man to have dominion over all things of the earth—in fact, to rule the world for His sake, and to subdue all things back to His feet (1:28).

Now the necessity for man to *subdue* the earth and all things in it was because of what God's enemy had done to it, the earth having now been put in opposition to its Creator. As was mentioned before, this world had been created by God according to His will and purpose. Now what was that will? Obviously, God's creation was not brought into existence for its own sake; on the contrary, God created it for His Son to be manifested. Indeed, each and every thing in the world was meant to express something of Christ Jesus, God's Son. However, today, we find the world and all things in it to be exactly the opposite. Instead of expressing Christ in all His beauty, the world is the expression of the enemy of God because

The World

Satan is a usurper who in ages past had become the prince of the world. But ultimately God's will and purpose cannot be defeated.

Now it needs to be repeated that God had first commissioned the recovery of the world back to His original purpose through man who was created in the image of God and after His likeness. And so, God had entrusted into man's hands the dominion over all things for the purpose of subduing them all back to the feet of God. But man failed in carrying out that commission due to his sin in the Edenic garden; and when he failed, the trust, rulership, and management of this world fell from the hands of man and into the hands of Satan.

Nevertheless, we must recognize the fact that though this transfer of rulership and management of the world took place due to man's failure, God as the Creator of all things never gave up His ownership of the world. What Satan took possession of from the hands of man was only the governing or ruling dominion over the world and everything in it. Satan simply became a usurper, and though he is called the prince of the world, he does not own the world. He thought he did, but he does not. The ownership has still remained in the hands of God, and He is going to regain and restore all things back to himself. And if one reads the Gospel of John carefully, it will become clear that the apostle John clearly understood all this.

In the olden days among the children of Israel, whenever there was to be a transaction of property, those involved had an open book which ultimately became a sealed book that was prepared in advance. All the conditions would be written down in that book but it would be sealed. And the person who received the property would gain possession of that sealed book. He would then open it to see all the conditions and understandings that were written therein.

So this scroll or book described in Revelation 5 represented the title deed to the property of the entire created world. The world and all things created are God's property, but the enemy is currently usurping it. Who, then, is worthy to drive out the enemy, to subdue all things, and bring them all back to God himself? Such a one must be immensely worthy in order to accomplish all this; nevertheless, nobody was found worthy enough—no angel, no man, no devil. And that is the reason John wept and kept on weeping because he saw that it was seemingly hopeless; all was lost: the world would never be recovered, there would be no restitution or the recovering of all things back to the purpose of God.

Now if you were John and—like him—understood the situation, would you not also weep, thinking that all was horribly hopeless? But John was comforted, for one of the elders said: "Weep not; there is One who is worthy. Behold, the Lion of the tribe of Judah, the Root of David, has overcome so as to open the book and its seven seals." Then John saw in the center of the throne, and encircled by the four living creatures and the twenty-four elders, a little Lamb standing, having been newly slain, and possessing seven horns and seven eyes which are the seven Spirits of God sent into all the earth. It came forward and took the book out of the right hand of Him that sat upon the throne—even God the Father. At that very moment the ownership of the world came into the hands of the Lord Jesus, who, as the slain Lamb, had overcome, having thus become the only one worthy to take the book, open its seals, and bring all things of recovery to pass. How we praise God for that!

Indeed, worship and praise immediately broke out, not only with the twenty-four elders and the four living creatures, but with thousands upon thousands upon thousands of angels. Not only that, all of creation—that is to say, all created things—began to worship the Lamb and to sing forth: "To Him who sits upon the throne and to the Lamb, blessing and honor, glory and might to the ages of ages."

When the Lord Jesus arrived back into heaven from the earth, He was the One who was worthy to take that book, to open it, and to bring all things back to the feet of God. And in

The World

view of that, it needs to be asked: What is the Lord Jesus doing in heaven today so far as the world is concerned? The answer is to be found in the fact that He is opening the seals of that book. According to God's plan the Lamb is executing the will of God in bringing the world and all things in it back to the feet of Him who sits on the Throne of Heaven. This is the work of the Lord Jesus in heaven today. Thank God that one day the kingdoms of this world will all become the kingdom of our God and of the Lord Jesus Christ (Revelation 11:15 AV), and this, we know, is to occur towards the end of this Age of Grace.

Knowing this is very important for believers because, as we look at the various things which are happening all around us, all of us, I believe, have a sense that the end is approaching. Moreover, as the people of the world observe all these things currently occurring and as they will observe the other things which are yet to occur, they shall become increasingly frightened nearly to death and shall become paralyzed as to what they should do (cf. Luke 21:26). This, however, ought not to be the case with us believers. For as the Lord Jesus himself had explained to His disciples, "When all these things commence taking place, you should lift up your heads, for your redemption is drawing nigh" (see Luke 21:28).

We thank God that all these things are not accidental. Though Satan tries his best to resist the giving up of his kingdom and hence the occurrence all over the world of numerous wars, rumors of war, and tribulations and sufferings of all kinds, nevertheless, we realize that the risen and ascended Lord Jesus as the slain Lamb of God is executing His Father's will: He is recovering the world back to its real owner—even His Father. The Bible therefore instructs us to "not be discouraged nor frightened" (see Joshua 1:9; cf. Luke 21:28). Though things shall get worse, though things shall happen which we could never imagine, even so, we can thank God, for we know who is at the back of all these terrible happenings—even God's archenemy, Satan—and who shall continue to manage all the world's affairs till he shall be totally defeated and God's kingdom shall come. Therefore, this aspect of the revelation of Jesus Christ as the slain Lamb of God upon the heavenly throne can give us believers assurance, confidence, and hope.

In view of all this that has been said, I would like, before concluding this message, for us to look more closely at the slain Lamb on the throne and at this matter of the seven seals. And to begin our consideration together, I would like to make inquiry about this: Upon our having observed the Lamb taking the book from His Father's hand, do any of us today think He would wait two thousand or more years before He would begin opening its seals? Inconceivable! Hence, it is my belief that upon His arrival in heaven and taking that book, He immediately began to open the seals.

Matthew 24 records the fact that Jesus' disciples had asked Him the following: "When will be Your return coming and the end of this world?" And Jesus explained as follows: "There will be false Christs and false prophets. There will be wars, famines, earthquakes, and similar such things, but the end is not yet. All this is but the beginning of birth pangs" (see vv. 3-8). In other words, as the Lord Jesus commences bringing all things back to God by opening the seals of His title deed to the world, there will be trauma. There will be all kinds of distress and opposition; for as was indicated earlier, the enemy, though having suffered a decisive defeat at Calvary, will not give up his usurpation easily but will do his utmost, by various tactics of his, to delay the date of the coming of God's kingdom. Yet, though there will be all kinds of tribulation, nevertheless, said Jesus, "All this is not negative since these shall be constituted the beginning of birth pangs"—meaning that out of these various troubles something will be born that will answer to God's heart and greatly please Him.

This is still the Age of Grace, yet, even now the Lord Jesus as the slain Lamb in the midst of the throne has begun His work

The World

of recovering all things back to God. How, though, has He been doing this work from heaven's throne? I believe the Lamb is already opening the seals of the title deed to the world to bring it back to the feet of His beloved Father. In fact, I personally believe that at least four seals have already been opened because they closely correspond with the content of Matthew 24. Indeed, it is my belief that it is because of this action by the Lord Jesus as the slain Lamb that from the time of Jesus' ascension even to our day there have been all these conflicts, wars, pestilences, destruction, death, false prophets and false teachers, and all such other kinds of things occurring throughout the world. In the eyes of man the world is not getting better nor reformed but is becoming worse and worse. Nevertheless, all of this is in the plan of God.

Moreover, it is my further belief that the fifth seal has begun to be opened, for from underneath the altar the souls of them that throughout the centuries have been slain for the word of God and for the testimony which they held, are seen crying out with a loud voice, saying: "How long, O sovereign Ruler, holy and true, dost thou not judge and avenge our blood on them that dwell upon the earth?" (see Revelation 6:9-10) In other words, with the opening of the fifth seal those who have become martyrs throughout the ages are heard crying out to God, "How long until You avenge us?"

Let us notice in this passage of Scripture that the tone of prayer has changed. What has heretofore been the tone of the martyrs' prayers up till today? The tone of their prayers throughout the Age of Grace can be likened to the prayer of the Lord Jesus: "Father, forgive them, for they know not what they do" (see Luke 23:34a). Likewise, the first Christian martyr, Stephen, had said, "Lord, do not hold this sin against them" (see Acts 7:60a). Such has been the prayer of the church and her martyrs throughout this centuries-old Age of Grace: "Forgive." But here in Revelation 6 the tone of their prayers has radically changed with the opening of the fifth seal. Instead of praying according to the character of forgiveness, they are here heard praying for vengeance to be meted out upon those on earth who had done them harm. Now that reveals that a change in time will have arrived with the opening of the fifth seal.

Then these martyrs were told: "Wait; wait a little longer until your fellow bondmen and their brethren, who were about to be killed as they had been, should be fulfilled" (see v. 11b). Are we aware that the martyrs of the twentieth century have been more in number than those of the first century? So we can assert with a good deal of confidence that the Age of Grace is nearing its end. We do not know with absolute certainty that the fifth seal has already been opened, but it is obvious and most certain that in coming to the sixth seal, we can clearly observe that God's judgment shall begin to come upon this world in earnest. Let us therefore pause and consider the description of this sixth seal more closely.

With the opening of the sixth seal we have revealed to us the wrath of the resurrected slain Lamb. Most often we think of a lamb as being patient, lowly, meek, self-sacrificing, and never becoming angry. Indeed, one can do most anything to a lamb, and it will only respond with meekness. Once I witnessed in New Zealand a competition among sheep-shearers to see who was the quickest in shearing the lambs. In their doing so, all the wool would come off each lamb in one piece. Because the shearers did their work so hurriedly, there was one lamb I saw whose ear had accidentally been cut off, but there was no sound which came forth from the lamb. There was merely a little jerking movement but no sound. That is the normal disposition of a lamb. But one day there will be manifested the *wrath* of the slain Lamb of God (Revelation 6:16c-17). Today, the world despises the Lord Jesus. It treats Him as though He is a nobody, and worth nothing, and there is only the patience of a lamb in response. But there is coming a day when the patience of the Lamb of God will be exhausted, and this world will experience "the great day of [His] wrath" (6:17a) as the Lamb. And when

The World

the resurrected slain Lamb becomes angry, "who can stand?" (6:17b) Indeed, we are told in verses 15 and 16 of Revelation 6 that this world's kings, princes, generals, the rich and mighty, and every slave and freeman will hide themselves in caves and among the mountain rocks and call out to the mountains and rocks: "Fall upon us and hide us from the wrath of the Lamb!"

We can discern from all this a new revelation of Jesus Christ, one which we have never seen or heard about before. The day is coming when the lion character of the Lamb shall appear, and when that happens, judgment will come upon this world in haste and severity. The world will end with judgment being poured out in order to purify it, but after its judgment, Christ's kingdom will be established upon this earth at last.

This should draw out from us much praise and worship to the Lamb of God!

Chapter Three

The Overcomers

He that has an ear, let him hear what the Spirit says to the assemblies [or, churches]. To him that overcomes, I will give to him to eat of the tree of life which is in the paradise of God.

Revelation 2:7

He that overcomes, to him will I give to sit with me in my throne; as I also have overcome, and have sat down with my Father in his throne. He that has an ear, let him hear what the Spirit says to the assemblies [or, churches].

Revelation 3:21-22

And I saw, and behold, the Lamb standing upon mount Zion, and with him a hundred and forty-four thousand, having his name and the name of his Father written upon their foreheads. And I heard a voice out of the heaven as a voice of many waters, and as a voice of great thunder. And the voice which I heard was as of harp-singers harping with their harps; and they sing a new song before the throne, and before the four living creatures and the elders. And no one could learn that song save the hundred and forty-four thousand who were bought from the earth. These are they who have not been defiled with women, for they are virgins: these are they who follow the Lamb wheresoever it goes. These have been bought from men as first-fruits to God and to the Lamb: and in their mouths was no lie found; for they are blameless.

Revelation 14:1-5

We have been considering together the prophetic book of Revelation and the key to its understanding—that being what we are told in its chapter 19: that "the spirit of prophecy is the testimony of Jesus" (v. 10e). And in our previous two sessions together we have come to see what the revelation of Jesus Christ is in relation to the church and also to the world. And today I would like for us to look at the revelation of Jesus Christ in relation to the overcomers of the church, and this matter is covered in chapters 1-19 of Revelation.

Back in the Old Testament times the glory of God had appeared to Abraham, and through Abraham He had called out a people to himself (Genesis 17:5-7). He later brought this people out of Egypt to Mount Sinai, and there he told them: "If you will keep My commandments and My covenant I will make you My people. Out of all the nations of the earth you will be Mine, and you will serve Me as a nation of priests" (see Exodus 19:4-6a). In other words, out of all peoples on the earth God had redeemed one particular people to himself, and He committed himself to them.

At that time in the world's history the entire earth's peoples were worshiping idols, but this particular chosen people—the Jews—were redeemed out of the world and were thus the only ones on earth who worshiped the one and only true God. They had His Law, His covenant, His tabernacle, and His temple; and His very name had been entrusted to them. Not only did God reveal himself to this people but He also committed himself to them in order that they might be His testimony to the world. Unfortunately, the children of Israel rebelled against God again and again until their nation and God's temple were destroyed and the Jewish people themselves taken captive and carried off to Babylon.

That did not mean, however, that God had lost His testimony upon the earth because we discover that He has had a strategy in reserve continually for whenever His people might fail. And there are those of us who have called that strategy the remnant principle. Furthermore, we must bear in mind that when the children of Israel as a nation were destroyed, God's name was no longer known and testified to on the earth. This we have come to know as a fact because during the days, months and years of the Jews' captivity He was called only the God of the heavens—never, the God of the heavens *and the earth*; for this was clearly due to the fact that during that lengthy period of His people's captivity He had no testimony upon the earth. But thank God, after seventy years of captivity a *remnant* of that failed people returned to Jerusalem. For though the majority of this people had settled themselves down comfortably in the land of captivity, contented and enjoying themselves, there was nonetheless a remnant altogether of fifty thousand people whom the Spirit of God had stirred and who returned to Jerusalem—a ruined place—to rebuild the temple of God so that He might once again have a name known upon the earth.

Let us clearly understand here that this was a remnant of *the whole nation*. For when they returned to this nation's capital, the first act they performed was to build an altar with twelve stones representative of all twelve tribes of Israel—a demonstration clearly of the remnant principle. When man failed and fell, God nonetheless resumed having His testimony on earth by means of a faithful remnant. Confirmation of this we find in what Ezra the priest had offered up to God in a prayer of thanksgiving and praise: "In thy mercy thou hast given us a remnant" (see Ezra 9:8).

When the children of Israel rebelled against God, that nation was temporarily set aside, and, so, God began to look upon the Gentiles. But that does not mean God's promises to Abraham or to Israel were canceled. Today, there are some who believe that the church is the new Israel and has taken over all the covenants and blessings which God had promised to Israel. Now I will not contest this interpretation with them, but so far as my understanding is concerned I feel that God who promised Abraham will always keep such promise. He will never alter it, change it, or transfer it to somebody else. So according to my understanding of the matter, even though Israel was temporarily set aside, I find the apostle Paul declaring in Romans 11 this: "Though Israel is today still set aside, that does not mean Israel has been permanently rejected, since I also am an Israelite" (see v. 1ff.). There is therefore a remnant according to grace (v. 5), and one day all Israel will be saved at the coming of the Lord (v. 26). All the promises which God had given to Abraham will be fulfilled, literally. So during Old Testament times the remnant principle was God's strategy. He knew how untrustworthy man was, but though man might fail Him He had His way of recovering all things.

We may thank God that today we are living under a new covenant—a covenant of grace—and we too are the people of God. Israel was His earthly physical people whereas we are His heavenly spiritual people; and so He has made a new covenant with us (cf. Hebrews 9:15). When the Lord Jesus saved us, He not only committed His name to us, He committed himself to us. In other words, the revelation of Jesus Christ is given to the church, and because He reveals himself to us, therefore, He has committed himself to us. And thus we have a responsibility to be His testimony in and to the world.

We can discern this to be the case from what is presented at the very beginning of the book of Acts where we read how the church was first formed on earth. The church began with just 120 believers, yet the glory of God was with them, for in one day alone 3,000 believers were added to the church, and they continued faithfully in the teaching and fellowship of the apostles, in the breaking of bread and prayers. The glory of the Lord was with them and His presence was so living. If there arose anything wrong among them, immediately discipline came upon them from above. They had problems but they became opportunities for the church to grow, because when the problems were solved according to God's wisdom, the name of the Lord Jesus continued to spread.

Let us also note that subsequently in the church at Antioch the believers were first called Christians. This came about because the world looked at the believers there and observed how different they were: some may have been Jews, some may have been Gentiles, yet they walked unitedly together in a way totally foreign to the world: they did not walk as Jews any longer, nor did they walk henceforth in the manner of Gentiles: they walked together in the way of the Lord, and thus it was a totally different manner of life. Moreover, it was not a way of living forced upon them but was that which came from within them. Indeed, the presence of the Lord was with them and it was therefore quite real. And that is what the church ought to be.

Now in our consideration together today of the subject of overcomers, I believe we all must acknowledge that the Lord Jesus is *the* overcomer. When that mighty angelic voice rang out inquiring as to "who is worthy to take the book and open its seals," there was no one found worthy in heaven, on earth, or beneath the earth to take and open the book that was in the Father's right hand. However, the Lion of Judah, the Root of David, has overcome and is therefore worthy to take the book and open its seals and to execute God's will regarding the world. (Revelation 5:1-5).

We learn from Genesis that the first man Adam fell when he was tempted by Satan. And when man fell, the world which God had entrusted to his management fell with him. But then the second Man (I Corinthians 15:47) came to the earth: "The Word became flesh and tabernacled among men, full of grace and truth" (see John 1:14). And while He was on earth He was tempted—just as we are—but without having sinned. For after He was baptized the enemy tempted Him in the wilderness forty days and nights by means of everything with which man could ever be tempted; yet, the Lord Jesus overcame Satan in all his temptations. Moreover, throughout His life He overcame both adversity and even prosperity; for when people tried to lift Him up, He went to the mountain and prayed (John 6:14-15), and when people tried to persecute Him, He truly suffered. Nevertheless, Jesus overcame all the temptations, sufferings, and trials of this world.

For let it be understood that though He was a perfect man, He had a will just as do we. Ours, of course, is a fallen will, but His was an unfallen, perfect human will. And therefore, had He willed to do anything on His own He would not have sinned, whereas were we to do that, we would definitely sin. Throughout Jesus' life on earth He overcame as a man: He never *spoke* anything out from himself, He never *did* anything out from himself, and He never *went* anywhere according to His will or thought (see, e.g., John 5:19, 30; 7:6, 8-10; 8:28; 12:49-50; 14:10, 24, 31). Throughout His entire earthly life the Son of man denied himself and obeyed the Father—Jesus was, in short, a perfect man; for He overcame the world, He overcame Satan, He overcame sin on the cross, and He overcame even himself as a man. There can be no doubt that Jesus is *the* overcomer, and because of that, He is worthy to execute God's will concerning this world as reflected in His opening the seven seals of the book which He as the slain Lamb received from the hand of Him who sits on the heavenly throne.

Hence, we who believe in the Lord Jesus are likewise supposed to be overcomers because I John 5 declares: "Those who believe in the Lord Jesus as the Son of God overcome the world, and they overcome the world by their faith" (see vv. 4-5). We who believe in the Lord Jesus are therefore expected to be overcomers. For are we not twice-born so as to be able to be overcomers because we receive an overcoming life—even the eternal life of the Lord Jesus that is within us? Now that is a speaking of this matter in the individual sense; yet, even when speaking in the corporate sense in terms of the church, we dare to speak of the church triumphant because of the total overcoming victory of Christ in His having disarmed the demonic powers and authorities and in His having made a public spectacle of them by means of the cross (Colossians 2:13). In Jesus having overcome every one of God's enemies, all twice-born believers enter into the reality of His overcoming. Therefore, the church on earth is supposed to be the church triumphant, overcoming sin, the world, self and the flesh—and even God's enemies, which are the evil forces. *That* in God's eyes is what the church is. And thank God that at the beginning of church history it was indeed the church triumphant. And, as the early church followed Christ she lived victoriously. Let us ever be mindful, however, that in this fallen human flesh of ours there is no good (Romans 7:18a); for even with all the salvation, provision, and life which God has given us, whenever something of the goodness of God comes into our hands we may quickly spoil it.

In his letter of I Timothy, which was written in the early 'sixties of the first century A.D., Paul opined as follows regarding the church: "The church is the base and pillar of truth. It is the church of the living God. It is the greatness of the mystery of godliness" (see 3:15-16). That is how the apostle was wont to describe the church *then*. By the time of the *late* 'sixties, however, Paul was led to describe the church quite differently; for in his II Timothy letter Paul was inspired by the Spirit to write this: "There is a great house, and in that great house there will be vessels to honor and vessels to dishonor, vessels of gold and vessels of clay. Now if you sanctify yourself from being the vessel of dishonor, then you will be fit for the Master's use" (see 2:20-21).

We can therefore infer from this Scripture passage that even as early as the first century's late 'sixties, we find that the church had gradually departed from Christ; and whenever there is a departure from Christ, there will be a departure from victory. The church by that time had gradually descended into becoming simply a great house full of mixture: there were vessels to honor and vessels to dishonor, wooden and earthen vessels, golden and silver vessels; and the call went out to sanctify and cleanse one's self from being a vessel of dishonor. In other words, if a person is no longer willing to remain a vessel of dishonor but is now truly desirous of becoming a vessel of honor to the Lord, then that one can do it by sanctifying or setting himself apart from what is of man and from what is base and mean and can seek the Lord and become a vessel of honor, serviceable and fit for the Master's use. And once again this idea of remnant makes its appearance.

With reference in the New Testament era to God's people who are today the church, God in His word has employed a new term: that of *overcomers* and no longer *remnant*, though the concept is exactly the same. Therefore, when we come to the book of Revelation, whose date of writing by the apostle John is towards the *end* of the first century, the call to *overcome* came into the church. When the Lord Jesus was on earth, He called for disciples—those who believed in Him—to follow Him. But now He calls His disciples or His church to overcome because of the general spiritual declension which has occurred among God's people. Though God's people have been saved by grace they have not gone on faithfully with the Lord. They have not grown up and matured but have remained as babes (cf. I Corinthians 3:1-2). They have continued to live according to the flesh and not according to the Spirit (cf. Romans 8:4ff.), and because of this they have been overcome instead of having been overcomers. That is why in the last days the call of God to His people is the call to overcome.

We are currently living in the day of declension. No, actually, to be more accurate, we are living towards the end of it, and ever since that call came from the Lord at the end of the first century, that same call has continued to be sounded right up to our own day. The seven letters to the seven churches in Asia Minor which we find laid out in Revelation chapters 2 and 3 were the risen, ascended Lord's letters sent to His church towards the end of the first century, and He issued those letters to the church as a whole. But let us notice that at the conclusion of each and every letter He announced: "He that has an ear, let him hear what the Spirit says to the churches. To him that overcomes ..."

But let us also notice that at the beginning of each letter we find what turns out to be a *partial* description of the Lord himself. Whereas in chapter 1 there is a *full* vision of the risen and ascended Lord as the royal High Priest, in each of the seven letters there is only one part, facet or aspect of the total revelation of the Lord Jesus that was presented in the first chapter. In other words, the Lord Jesus committed himself to the church as a whole, but to each local assembly there is a measure or degree of His revelation, a measure or degree of His commitment, and a measure or degree of the testimony that those in that assembly should hold forth and maintain for Him. And, thus, when one brings the whole church into view, there will be a full revelation of Jesus Christ and a full testimony to the world because the church is one. No assembly possesses it all, but each assembly is special and has a particular commitment of the Lord based upon the measure of revelation given to it. Therefore, according to the measure of His revelation of himself, there will be the measure or degree of His commitment, and such becomes the measure of each assembly's testimony to the world concerning the Lord Jesus.

The letter issued by the Lord to each of these seven churches begins with a revelation of himself to that church, and then as the royal High Priest He follows that up by looking into each of the golden lampstands to see what is the condition of that particular assembly and whether He can find himself there. The Lord Jesus has revealed himself to each local assembly, and in accordance with that partial revelation of himself He is now coming into the midst of these assemblies to look for himself there: He is looking to see whether the believers in this and that assembly are being faithful to the particular revelation He had given of himself—that is to say, whether those believers are responding to His revelation of himself in such manner that it is now their vocation and that they are thus living it out as a testimony to the world concerning himself. Sad to say, however, when the risen, ascended Lord came to each assembly and to the church as a whole, He could barely find himself.

There is a marvelous story concerning A. J. Gordon who was the pastor of a church in Boston, Massachusetts USA. He greatly loved the Lord, and that particular church assembly was blessed through him. He once had a dream. While he was sitting on the platform waiting for the moment to stand and begin to preach, he saw a stranger walk in and the usher lead him to a seat. Somehow that stranger attracted the attention of brother Gordon; so much so, that during all the time he was preaching he was inwardly wondering who that stranger was, and oh, how he would like to meet and come to know him. The custom of the pastor after the sermon was finished was for him to go to the main door of the church building and greet everybody as they filed out; and hence, brother Gordon wanted very much to take this opportunity to greet that person. But by the time the pastor had arrived at the door, the person had vanished; so he asked the usher: "Who was that person?" And the usher said, "Don't you know Him? It was Jesus. Jesus came to church today." And brother Gordon began to fear: "What did He think of my sermon? What did He think of the pipe organ? What did He think of the choir? What did He think of these and other things? Did He approve? Was He happy? Or was He unhappy about it?" And from that moment forward that dream of his changed A. J. Gordon completely in his relationship with the Lord.

Let us not think that Christ will not come to us. He may even be here with us today. What will He think about us? An assembly of His people may have all the good, commendable, and religious things. Let us be reminded, however, that the Lord saw all such things in every Asia Minor church among those seven mentioned in Revelation, but these were *things* and not himself. It was not His revelation of himself nor was it what He was looking for. Nothing can satisfy Him unless He sees His self—His divine nature—in His people.

When, for instance, He came to the church in Ephesus, He found all kinds of good things—work, labor, knowledge, truth—and yet, He could not find himself as the people's first love. That is what He desires—love with all one's heart, mind, and strength. That *agape* love of His was not there. Yes, the work was there, the labor was there, the endurance was there, the knowledge was there—but the Lord himself was not there.

When He next came to the church in Smyrna, He encouraged the believers there to be faithful to the point of death. They definitely had been faithful up to that point, but they would be tested ten more days; and so they were exhorted to be faithful even to death because He is the one who had died and is risen. That was His revelation of himself to them. That is what He is, and He wants His church to be what He is also.

Then the risen, ascended Lord came to the church in Pergamos, where He found that they had been faithful in the beginning but they had begun departing from the truth. He had looked for truth because He is the truth (John 14:6a).

When He came to the church in Thyatira, He found a depth of Satan there. They had lost the simplicity that is to be found in Christ (II Corinthians 11:3). And hence, He looked for that simplicity but found it was not there.

Upon next coming to the assembly in Sardis, the Lord found that there was a lack of living faith among the believers there. In name she was alive but in reality there was no life there, and He is the life that was expected to be manifested among them.

In the church at Philadelphia, praise God, the Lord of love had finally found himself because He saw that brotherly love was greatly manifested among the brethren there (cf. John 13:34-35). They also had not denied His name and had kept His word of patience. This has always been the day of patience for God's people during the Age of Grace.

Finally, in coming to the Laodicean assembly the Lord Jesus found no reality there whatsoever. Everything was superficial and that which was completely other than himself. Because there was no spiritual reality present, He found it necessary to place himself outside the door of this church's believers' hearts and knock to gain needful entrance.

Such, then, was the condition of the church at the end of the first century. But let us thank and praise God that though the majority of the believers had failed, there was an overcoming remnant in the church. They were those who had an ear to hear what the Spirit was and is still saying to the churches, and they responded positively to the call to overcome.

Throughout the book of Revelation we are given to see overcomers in the church; in fact, they have been manifested throughout the history of the church. In Revelation, for instance, in its chapter 7 we read: "After these things I saw, and lo, a great crowd, which no one could number, out of every nation and tribe and people and tongue, standing before the throne, and before the Lamb, clothed with white robes, and palm branches in their hands" (v. 9).

Who are these people? If we read Revelation in accordance with the factor of time, we can conclude that they are the overcomers of the church dating from the second century up to the moment approaching the time for the return of the Lord. Therefore, we behold a great crowd which no one can number. We must praise God for that. In every century—from the second to the twenty-first in our own day—God has not failed to have His overcomers. Though the majority of God's people have failed, God has not failed. He has a great multitude of overcomers which when totaled cannot be counted.

So whenever the church as a whole has departed from the truth and from the faith, there has always been a small number who were faithful to the revelation of Jesus Christ, and who followed the Lamb wheresoever He went (Revelation 14:4b). They had their robes made white by the blood of the Lamb (Revelation 7:14c). They have not been people who were superior to the other believers, but one thing they all have had: a knowledge of the preciousness of the blood of the Lord Jesus (Revelation 7:14c, 12:11a). They have not been perfect for they have had their moments of failure; nevertheless, they have been those who have clung to the Lamb and have been washed with His blood. They have been those who have maintained a living relationship with Christ and have accepted the heavenly intercessory ministry of Christ to themselves (Hebrews 7:25b). They have been those who have drawn near to Him and been saved to the uttermost by Him (Hebrews 7:25a).

Let us notice too that in Revelation 12 there is a vision which John saw of a woman in travail to give birth and of an enormous red dragon that is waiting there before her. Please note that at this moment the dragon is not at all interested in the woman, he is only interested in what is in the woman's womb. Of course, people have different interpretations, and I shall not attempt to impose my own interpretation upon you, since the letter of the word kills (II Corinthians 3:6). I only wish for us to catch the spirit of this heavenly vision. But let us suppose that this woman represents the church at the end time—that is, in our time. Satan the dragon is not interested in, nor is threatened by, the church at the end time because he well knows she in her degenerate state can do nothing to him, for the church is now quite weak and has—in apostasy—gravely departed from truth, life, and love that are to be found in Christ. Indeed, she is within his grasp already, so the Dragon/Satan is not concerned about the church at this time. But he *is* concerned about the content of that woman's womb: What this interpretation of the vision is therefore intimating is, that the church is in great travail. In other words, we who comprise the church are being shaken in travail for the purpose of producing that which will please the Lord; and, therefore, this travailing of the church is not a suffering for the sake of suffering but is unto something quite purposeful and meaningful.

Let us be clear here that we who make up the church are in the day of great shaking. Everywhere we may go, in every gathering of God's people, we cannot help but observe a shaking of the church taking place that goes to the very core of her existence. We may even think that the church will simply collapse into nothing and end up as being over and done with; but no, through the church's travail God is bringing forth a manchild who represents all the overcomers at the end-time; for it is clear from Scripture that the man-child possesses a collective identity, in that verse 11 describes him thus: "*They* overcame him [the accuser of the brethren] by the blood of the Lamb and by the word of their testimony, and they loved not their lives even unto death."

By noticing Satan's intense interest in devouring the manchild when born, we can conclude that God's enemy well knows that this man-child—the overcomers of the church—would be able to fulfill the mission which Christ had given to the entire church to accomplish. And they do so—not for themselves but on behalf of the whole church. They would be but the firstfruits that if successfully caught up to heaven despite Satan's intended interference will guarantee the entire harvest of believing souls (Revelation 14:4c).

Now they are described as those who overcome by the blood of the Lamb—for they are not perfect but have their failures like everybody else; yet, they continually come to the Lord and receive His intercessory ministry, and He thus saves them completely (Hebrews 7:25). And these overcomers also bear a great testimony to the world because they are the ones who manifest the testimony of Jesus, they not only maintaining the testimony but also *voicing* it (Revelation 12:11b). Furthermore, they do not love their soul-life even to the point of death (Revelation 12:11c): Indeed, they follow the Lamb wheresoever He goes (Revelation 14:4b).

Thus, the overcomers shall constitute the welcoming party who shall escort the Lord Jesus to the earth when He returns (cf. Luke 21:36). Those who are overcomers are not waiting for death but are waiting to be taken—that is, to be raptured. That, in fact, is their blessed hope.

Then in chapter 15 of Revelation there is another vision: "And I saw as a glass sea, mingled with fire, and those that had gained the victory over the beast, and over its image, and over the number of its name, standing upon the glass sea, having harps [given them] of God" (v. 2). These, in my view, are the overcomers during the period of the Great Tribulation. Even in that extremely difficult period there will be overcomers who refuse to have the number of the beast upon them. They refuse to worship the idol—the beast—and they are martyred.

We may conclude, therefore, that throughout the ages God will have His overcomers who carry on the testimony of Jesus. The reason they overcome is because Christ himself has overcome and they possess and manifest His overcoming life. We can never overcome by ourselves, but if we follow Him and trust Him, we will receive His enabling supply and His needful ministry, and we shall be more than conquerors even in the midst of difficulty, trial, and testings of every kind (Romans 8:35-37). For those who are overcomers know who is on the throne of heaven—even Jesus the Lamb of God, who had himself overcome when on earth.

And hence, the Lord Jesus is working out that which is most precious to Him. He is shaking His church by means of allowing sorrows, trials, failures, defeats, tears, and wounds to come upon believers—and all for the purpose of bringing forth a man-child: those collectively who are maturing in Christ Jesus and are becoming the overcomers of the church. When we are saved, we are all babes in Christ and can assume no responsibility. What the Lord is therefore looking for are many matured and trained brethren who can eventually share with Him not only His glory but also His responsibility in the coming kingdom. Consequently, for the purpose of maturing His saints the Lord arranges for them to go through all kinds of so-called adverse circumstances of life in order to discipline, mature and train them into becoming overcomers who will be a part of the man-child spoken of in Revelation 12.

I have often thought how precious it would have been at the moment I was saved had I been raptured to heaven. That would have spared me from having to experience all the aforementioned sorrows, trials, temptations, and oppositions of the enemy. But the Lord knows better: He is using all such circumstances to bring us into maturity so that we may be grown-up sons and daughters of God; for it is God's will that we be conformed to the image of His beloved Son (Romans 8:29a). The only begotten Son of God is destined to be the firstborn among many brethren (8:29b) and to lead many sons into glory (Hebrews 2:10a). Therefore, all is not negative or simply to be accounted as loss; instead, God the Father through His Son is working out something most wonderful and precious in the midst of all these trials and problems.

May God therefore help each one of us to be what He desires us to be: one of the Lord's many overcomers.

Chapter Four

The Millennium and Eternity

And I heard as a voice of a great crowd, and as a voice of many waters, and as a voice of strong thunders, saying, Hallelujah, for the Lord our God the Almighty has taken to himself kingly power. Let us rejoice and exult, and give him glory; for the marriage of the Lamb is come, and his wife has made herself ready. And it was given to her that she should be clothed in fine linen, bright and pure; for the fine linen is the righteousnesses of the saints. And he says to me, Write, Blessed are they who are called to the supper of the marriage of the Lamb. And he says to me, These are the true words of God. And I fell before his feet to do him homage. And he says to me, See thou do it not. I am thy fellow-bondman, and the fellow-bondman of thy brethren who have the testimony of Jesus. Do homage to God. For the spirit of prophecy is the testimony of Jesus.

Revelation 19:6-10

And I saw a new heaven and a new earth; for the first heaven and the first earth had passed away, and the sea exists no more.

And I saw the holy city, new Jerusalem, coming down out of the heaven from God, prepared as a bride adorned for her husband. And I heard a loud voice out of the heaven, saying, Behold, the tabernacle of God is with men, and he shall tabernacle with them, and they shall be his people, and God himself shall be with them, their God. And he shall wipe away every tear from their eyes; and death shall not exist any more, nor grief, nor cry, nor distress shall exist any more, for the former things have passed away. And he that sat on the throne said, Behold, I make all things new. And he says to me, Write, for these words are true and faithful. And he said to me, It is done. I am the Alpha and the Omega, the beginning and the end. I will give to him that thirsts of the fountain of the water of life freely. He that overcomes shall inherit these things, and I will be to him God, and he shall be to me son.

Revelation 21:1-7

In our three previous sessions of fellowship together concerning the Bible's concluding book—The Revelation of Jesus Christ—we have considered the revelation of the Lord Jesus in relation to the church, to the world, and to the overcomers of the church. And in our final session today, I would like for us to consider together the revelation of Jesus Christ in relation to the immediate Age to Come—known generally as the millennium—and to the Ages of Ages to come thereafter—which we call Eternity. We find this revealed in the last few chapters of the book of Revelation. In order to better understand what God has been doing and will continue to do in bringing to fruition His eternal purpose, we need to have some insight into the administration of God.

To that end, let us begin by realizing that even before the foundation of the world, God had purposed a purpose in himself, and that according to the good pleasure of His will He had laid out a plan or means of administration or method of management by which to fully execute His will. Apropos of this, we find the following explanation given by the apostle Paul in Ephesians 1:9-10: "Having made known to us the mystery of his will, according to his good pleasure which he purposed in himself for the administration of the fullness of times; to head up all things in the Christ, the things in the heavens and the things upon the earth."

This passage of Scripture tells us that before the foundation of the world God had purposed something in himself, from which we can conclude that whatever God does is never by chance, that in order to bring that purpose into fulfillment He had devised or thought up a way or method of administration or management. By creating and using time as His instrument, God has gradually and progressively been bringing all things to completion during time and according to His counsel and way of management. And when all things in the heavens and upon the earth have been brought to completion, all such things will be headed up, summed up, gathered up in Christ Jesus—with nothing being excepted!

Now with that as background, let us attempt to understand what is God's way or method by which He manages and administers everything. How does He bring all heavenly and earthly things to fruition and in accordance with His will and purpose? By reading and studying God's word we come to see His wisdom, His knowledge, and His ways. Some people refer to such understanding of God's ways as dispensation theology, and there are several different ideas or descriptions concerning this. Some hold to an extreme position of dispensationalism, while others do not believe in any form of dispensation at all.

What, then, is meant by the term dispensation when used in reference to God and His way of administration? Dispensation simply means a period of time that is set aside by God for a specific working out of His will. And when God is working out His will and purpose, He employs time and divides it into certain periods of emphasis. For during each period there is something special He wishes to do and/or accomplish by means of His administration, management, or discipline. In the Bible we will discover that there are very clear indications of these periods of time within which God has worked out His purpose.

For instance, Romans 5:14 says: "death reigned from Adam until Moses, even upon those who had not sinned in the likeness of Adam's transgression, who is the figure of him to come." This period from Adam to Moses is the first dispensation or stage in God's administration, and during that entire period death reigned. Now the reason death reigned is because of sin. But so far as the carrying out of God's will and purpose is concerned God is positive and not negative regarding that reign of death because that same period constituted simultaneously the dispensation of promise—God gave promise after promise. Immediately after man fell into sin God gave man a promise: the seed of the woman will crush the head of the serpent and the serpent will crush his heel (Genesis 3:16). God also promised Abraham that the seed of the woman would be coming and that thus there would be victory and recovery (Genesis 17:6-7). As one therefore reads on in God's word, from the moment of Adam to that of Moses there was promise after promise being given by God to man. That was God's first dispensational period, with an emphasis on promise.

That first period of time was followed by another, which manifested itself from the life of Moses to that of John the Baptizer. The Biblical source for this is to be found in Matthew 11:13: "all the prophets and the law have prophesied unto John." John the Baptizer, of course, was the forerunner of Christ. He was the concluding prophet of the Old Testament era and the herald of the New Testament age. During this second period or dispensation God again had His working plan, and it was characterized as being the dispensation of Law. In one sense this Age of Law *prepared the way* for the Age of Grace. We talk very much about Grace, but as a matter of fact if we are not sufficiently conversant with Law we will not appreciate Grace. Law serves as a tutor that leads us to Christ who is "full of grace" (Galatians 3:24a, John 1:14b). So during this dispensational period from Moses till the coming of John the Baptizer there was the administration of Law. It was as though God chose to place man under Law in order that man might learn to truly know himself and realize how much the grace of God was needed and how much man was equally in need of the Savior.

Following that second phase of time there came forth the third stage in the working out of God's purpose, and its timespan dates from the first coming of Christ to His second coming to the earth. This we find succinctly delineated for us in Paul's brief statement in II Corinthians 6: "Now is the time of salvation" (see v. 2b). There is a distinct time term stated here: *now*, which is this current age in which we find ourselves. When the Lord Jesus was about to ascend back to the Father, He instructed His disciples thusly: "Go to the world and disciple all nations, baptizing them in the name of the Father, the Son, and the Holy Spirit, and teach them all things that I have taught you, and I will be with you until the end of this age" (see Matthew 28:19-20). Hence, from the first coming of Christ to His return coming to the earth there is the dispensational period which we call the Age of Grace: "The Word became flesh, and tabernacled among men, full of grace and truth" (see John 1:14). Thank God that we are still living in this Age. Nevertheless, I believe we are approaching its end. Yes, this is the day of the patience of Christ; but one day soon this gracious Age will pass away, and it will be followed by yet another period: the dispensation of the Age to Come.

Jesus alluded to that Age in this particular assertion of His: "If you sin against the Holy Spirit, you will not be forgiven in this age nor in the coming age" (see Matthew 12:32). Also Hebrews 6 declares that some people have already tasted the powers of the Age to Come (v. 5). Accordingly, we can rightfully conclude that there will be another age ushered in after the conclusion of this current grace age, and this immediately coming new age is usually referred to as the millennium because this next age is destined to last a thousand years. And we are told in Revelation that after this thousand-year period is over there will occur the final rebellion of God's enemy, following which will come Eternity or the Ages of Ages that shall be characterized by the new heaven and the new earth and the new Jerusalem. Only with the coming of the Ages of the Ages shall redeemed mankind realize that the administration of God shall have fulfilled and completely executed His eternal purpose. And that is what I would like for us to consider together today.

What are God's people waiting for today? What is our blessed hope? We are looking forward to the return coming to the earth of the Lord Jesus. But I think there is much misunderstanding among God's people concerning His coming. As a matter of fact, there are many hymns which we sing that are scripturally incorrect. Christians often sing about the Lord's coming again in terms of His arriving with His angels in a cloud and as the trumpet is sounded all believers—both living and dead—are immediately gathered or raptured together to Him, with all this occurring as one single event in one moment of time.

However, I believe such an understanding is rather faulty. This is because the original New Testament Greek term *parousia* employed in the relevant New Testament passages—but especially in the two Pauline Thessalonian letters—and translated into English as "coming" can also be translated as "presence." For in this word *parousia*, *para* means "with" or "together" and *ousia* means "to be" or "being": thus conveying the overall meaning of "presence." Thus, this Greek term includes in its meaning the idea of arrival, and hence, that involves a presence. In fact, we are told, by those who know the New Testament Greek language well, that this term *parousia* in the original Greek, along with its English counterpart word "presence," convey the concept of a period of time covering a *series of events* and not just one event.

The Millennium and Eternity

Now if that be true, how will the Lord Jesus come back to the earth? That can be explained quite simply. By carefully reading Acts chapter 1 we are given to see at one moment the resurrected Jesus on the Mount of Olives with His Galilean disciples, and then God took Him. His feet left the Olivet mountain and He began ascending as His disciples looked up at Him. They saw Jesus gradually ascend and subsequently thereafter a cloud enveloped Him, thus hiding Him from their sight. Yet, though they could no longer see Jesus because of the cloud, they nonetheless continued looking up. So two men in white suddenly appeared and said: "Men of Galilee, why are you looking up? The One who is taken up from you into heaven will come back in the same way as you have seen Him go into heaven" (see vv. 9-11).

So what is the way Jesus went up? He clearly went up in two distinct stages. The first stage was from Olivet to the cloud—visible; the second stage was from the cloud to the throne—invisible. So the way of His coming back to earth will be the exact *reverse* of His ascending. And corresponding to these two reversed stages—one invisible, the other visible—Jesus, as recorded in Matthew 24, gave two different signs to His disciples regarding His coming again. One sign would be that He would come like a thief in the night (vv. 42-44), which thus corresponds and relates to the first of these reversed stages of His return coming: the risen, ascended Lord Jesus shall descend from the throne to the cloud in the air. So let us ask ourselves: Would a thief sound a trumpet announcing that he is coming? Obviously not; for he wishes to come secretly and unexpectedly to steal one's treasure and not one's trash. Hence, Jesus will come again to the earth but like a thief—*invisibly* descending, initially, from the throne to the cloud—and steal away that which answers to, and is the treasure of, His heart.

And the second sign Jesus gave His disciples concerning His coming again we find in verses 27, 30a, c: "as the lightning goes forth from the east and shines to the west, so shall be the coming of the Son of man. ... And then shall appear the sign of the Son of man in heaven; ... and they shall see the Son of man coming on the clouds of heaven with power and great glory." Thus Jesus' return coming will be seen by everyone: He will break through the cloud and *visibly* descend to the earth, with His feet touching down upon the Mount of Olives (Zechariah 14:4). Everybody will accordingly see Him because in this second stage of His return coming to earth He will be visible to all.

We therefore come to understand that actually the return coming of the Lord commences with the invisible stage covering His movement from the throne down to the cloud in the air. That helps to explain why we find in Revelation 12 that the woman mentioned there is in travail, she symbolizing the church as being in travail to give birth to a man-child, and as soon as that man-child is born, immediately he is caught up to the throne. Now in order for someone to go from earth to God's throne, which is situated in the third and highest heaven, that one must be able to break through the air which is the headquarters of Satan today (cf. Ephesians 6:12, Revelation 12:7-9). Hence, anyone who can break through Satan's headquarters must most certainly be an overcomer who has already overcome and who is able to go through enemy territory and reach the throne of heaven.

What will happen at the return coming of the Lord? We learn from the lips of Jesus himself as recorded in Matthew 24:37-41 and Luke 17:26-27, 34; 21:34-36 that His coming will be like what apparently occurred in the days of Noah at the time of the Universal Flood: two men were working out in the field at noontime, two women were grinding meal for the morning breakfast, and two men were sleeping at night; then, suddenly, in each instance, one was taken and the other was left behind; and the word *taken* in the Greek original here has the same meaning as was described in Acts in narrating what occurred when Jesus was taken up from His disciples into heaven (1:9a, 11b).

The Millennium and Eternity

So how does the return coming of the Lord begin? What events will mark or characterize that beginning? Please be advised that the Lord can come at any time. Let us not think that there are some prophecies still to be fulfilled before He can come. Not so, for all the prophecies concerning His return coming have already been fulfilled. It is quite true, of course, that there are other prophecies yet waiting to be fulfilled *at the moment of the coming of the Lord* and *after* His coming, but all the prophecies which we know of that are related to events which must occur *before* the beginning of *parousia* have all been fulfilled. We are therefore living in a very thrilling time. Those of us whose hearts are faithful towards the Lord Jesus are not here waiting to die but are waiting to be raptured alive. If we have been waiting, watching, praying, and following the Lamb wheresoever He goes (Revelation 14:4b), then before His arriving at the cloud from heaven's throne, He will steal you and me away, because if we have been faithful and are ready, then we are the treasure of His heart, and that constitutes the *beginning* of *parousia*: one believer will be taken up—raptured—while the other shall be left behind to be disciplined and further dealt with by the Lord.

The man-child of Revelation 12 already mentioned is a collective term because in referring a few verses later to the man-child, the plural pronoun "they" is employed: *"They overcame Satan by the blood of the Lamb, by the word of their testimony, and have not loved their life even unto death"* (see v. 11). So once those saints comprising the man-child have been snatched up to God and have arrived at His throne, the passage continues by stating that war would immediately break out in the air between the archangel Michael and his angels and Satan and his followers, with the result that the air—Satan's headquarters—shall be cleared of Satan and his angels, all of whom shall be thrown down upon the earth (vv. 7-9). This thus clears the air for the risen and ascended Lord Jesus to descend from God's throne to the cloud in the air. Meanwhile, the trio of evil—Satan, the Beast, and the False Prophet—shall all be together on the earth; and hence, what can anyone expect the situation on earth to be but the Great Tribulation!

Now after the three and a half years of immense tribulation, the Lord will descend from the air to the earth; the trumpet will sound, and all who are dead in Christ Jesus will be raised; while those who still remain alive on the earth will be changed, and all will be taken up to the air to meet the Lord. That will be the time of the judgment seat of Christ (II Corinthians 5:10) when all those in Christ shall appear before Him for Him to decide who of them are to inherit the kingdom of the heavens and reign with Him during the thousand years, and who of them are disqualified—though they shall indeed be "saved," but barely saved (see I Corinthians 3:15). And when the feet of the Lord touches the Olivet mount it will be broken into two (Zechariah 14:4), thus enabling His chosen people Israel to escape from surrounded Jerusalem and be saved.

The Bible has spoken much concerning the Messianic kingdom which God had promised to Abraham and the children of Israel. God had chosen them and committed himself to them. Unfortunately, they failed, resulting in Israel having been temporarily set aside, thus enabling the Gentiles to begin coming into the grace of God. But down through the centuries since being set aside there has always been a faithful remnant among the children of Israel, and God's will cannot be defeated. All the promises of God to Israel *will* be fulfilled.

Let us be reminded that in the Old Testament can be found many prophecies concerning this Messianic kingdom which speaks of the Messiah who is to come. In fact, punctuating these prophecies is the declaration that Israel will ultimately be made the first among all the nations, and she will become a nation of priests who will go forth to the other nations to declare the glory of God.

For instance, Isaiah 2:1-4 says:

The Millennium and Eternity

The word that Isaiah the son of Amoz saw concerning Judah and Jerusalem. And it shall come to pass in the end of days, that the mountain of Jehovah's house shall be established on the top of the mountains, and shall be lifted up above the hills; and all the nations shall flow unto it. And many peoples shall go and say, Come, and let us go up to the mountain of Jehovah, to the house of the God of Jacob; and he will teach us of his ways, and we will walk in his paths. For out of Zion shall go forth the law, and Jehovah's word from Jerusalem. And shall judge among the nations, and shall reprove many peoples; and they shall forge their swords into ploughshares, and their spears into pruning-knives: nation shall not lift up sword against nation, neither shall they learn war any more.

Similarly, Isaiah 11:1-10 declares:

And there shall come forth a shoot out of the stock of Jesse, and a branch out of his roots shall be fruitful; and the Spirit of Jehovah shall rest upon him, the spirit of wisdom and understanding, the spirit of counsel and might, the spirit of knowledge and of the fear of Jehovah. And his delight will be in the fear of Jehovah; and he shall not judge after the sight of his eyes, neither reprove after the hearing of his ears; but with righteousness shall he judge the poor, and reprove with equity the meek of the earth: and he shall smite the earth with the rod of his mouth, and with the breath of his lips shall he slay the wicked. And righteousness shall be the girdle of his reins, and faithfulness the girdle of his loins. The wolf also shall dwell with the lamb, and the leopard shall lie down with the kid, and the calf and the young lion and the fatted beast together, and a little child shall lead them. And the cow and the she-bear shall feed; their young ones shall lie down together; and the lion shall eat straw like the ox. And the sucking child shall play on the hole of the adder, and the weaned child shall put forth its hand to the viper's den. They shall not hurt nor destroy in all my holy mountain; for the earth shall be full of the knowledge of Jehovah, as the waters cover the sea. And in that day there shall be a root of Jesse, standing as a banner of the peoples: the nations shall seek it; and his resting-place shall be glory.

There are many, many other such prophecies. When the children of Israel are in their last trauma, Messiah Jesus will come to deliver them, and they shall see Him (Zechariah 12:10). Currently, the children of Israel as a whole are still in unbelief. God has already begun to return to His people and that is why the nation of Israel has been reestablished back in the year 1948. But even to this current day, Israel as a nation is still in unbelief, and they will continue to suffer until the day when they shall look upon Him whom they had pierced (Zechariah 12:10 again). Then all Israel will repent and be saved (Zechariah chapters 12-14). In other words, the day is coming when the kingdom of the heavens shall at last appear upon the earth.

Even so, the people of God are very much confused about the kingdom of the heavens—the heavenly kingdom which Christ shall establish when He finally returns to earth. We wonder: How is it to be established? How is it to function? In relation to the kingdom, what will happen to us believers in Christ? At the outset I wish to state that though there have been many different interpretations put forth regarding the kingdom,

The Millennium and Eternity

my earnest desire today is to try to grasp hold of and present what to me is the *spirit* of it all.

First of all, therefore, let me say that for the sake of better understanding, the thousand-year kingdom can most likely be divided into two parts with respect to how it is to function and be managed. There is the heavenly part and there is the earthly part. The earthly part is the Messianic kingdom—when Israel will be saved and become the first of the nations and whose people will be God's priests who will go forth throughout the nations during that millennial era to declare the glory of God. All the promises God gave to Abraham will be literally, physically fulfilled. But this is not what I now wish for us to focus upon. I wish us to consider what will happen to us believers in Christ, and that brings us to the heavenly part of the millennial kingdom.

We know, of course, that during this millennial era Christ will reign as the King of kings and the Lord of lords, and Israel will acknowledge Him as their Messiah-King. But the Lord Jesus will reign above in heaven—not on the earth—for this is why it is called the kingdom of the *heavens*. And while He is reigning from above over the whole earth, He as the King of kings and Lord of lords shall have those alongside Him who will reign with Him.

Now who are these people who will reign with Him? It seems most clear to me that they are the overcomers of the church throughout the ages past. They are the ones who shall "reign with Christ for a thousand years " (see the end of v. 4 of Revelation 20) because while they were living on earth they had been *trained* to reign by what they had patiently endured as overcomers. They had become fit to reign and thus they will be rewarded to reign with Christ on the throne throughout this entire thousand-year period. But what shall be more wonderful for those overcomers will not be the privilege of co-reigning with Christ. No, what shall be more wonderful to them is what is to be found in Revelation 19 where is described not only the coming of God's kingdom but also the bride who has made herself ready. We read that it was given her to be radiantly clothed with white, bright linen—signifying the righteousnesses of the saints—and that the marriage feast of the Lamb has come and that those who have been invited to attend it shall be greatly blessed.

Therefore, for those who are overcomers, they shall come to realize that it is not their reigning with Christ for which they are looking and waiting; rather, it is the Bridegroom—even Christ Jesus himself. In fact, it shall be during the time of the millennium that the Lord Jesus shall finally be able to assume His rightful place as the Bridegroom. When He first came to the earth, Jesus indeed came as a bridegroom searching for His bride, but He could not find her. He could only find the sick, the blind, the crippled, the dead, and those who either opposed Him or rejected Him. And hence, that is why He had to die, and from His side as He hung in death on the cross came forth water and blood (John 19:34), thus ushering in the Age of Grace for mankind. And so, just as Eve came out of the side of Adam (Genesis 2:21-23), so the church has come out of Jesus' side. And during this Age of Grace He is preparing His bride, getting her ready; but somehow, His bride still lingers. Oftentimes believers assume that they are the ones waiting—waiting for Christ, but it is more correct to say that Christ is the one waiting—waiting for us to be made ready and fit to be His bride. Is it not true that most likely you and I have never attended a wedding where the bride is waiting for the bridegroom? Instead, it is always the case that the bridegroom is waiting for the bride.

I know of only one instance in which the bride had to wait for the bridegroom. And here I'm referring to the bride of Hudson Taylor's great-grandfather. It so happened that as a young man, he turned out to be rather easygoing, and when he got up from bed on the morning of his wedding day, he suddenly realized he was to be married that very day and would soon have a family and that this would be a great responsibility.

The Millennium and Eternity

So he went out to a field to pray about this matter. He prayed and prayed and prayed, and in doing so he lost all sense of time. After he had prayed and had earnestly presented himself to God and His grace for what lay ahead in his life, he suddenly realized afresh that it was the day of his marriage, and that even now he was already late! The preacher was waiting, the guests were waiting, and of course the bride herself was waiting—all of them wondering where in the world the bridegroom was! And so he hurried off to the wedding place and was married, he being the only bridegroom I know of for whom the bride had to wait! (I might add, incidentally, that on their wedding night, this great-grandfather of Hudson Taylor told his newly-wedded wife: "Please kneel down and pray with me." That was a strange thing for this bride to hear, and she was completely taken by surprise. But as unusual as this entire incident turned out to be, we must nonetheless acknowledge that in looking at the history of this family of the Taylors, we find that one generation after another had ended up faithfully serving God.)

Yes, indeed, Christ is waiting for us to be made ready. Are we waiting for Him? Are we longing to see Him? It is not the rewards which ought to capture our vision; it is Christ Jesus himself who ought to do so. The eye of the bride of Christ is on the Bridegroom, and during the millennium He finally obtains His radiant bride who shares with Him in His glory.

However, when we come to Revelation chapter 21, we find that there is *another* bride in the new heaven and new earth. We see the new Jerusalem descending from heaven upon the earth and it is described as being a bride adorned for her husband. Is that not wonderful?!? So I would ask ourselves, Is it two weddings or one wedding? Is it two brides or one bride? Permit me to explain the matter in the following way, as best as I have been given to understand the matter.

During the *millennium* the Lord Jesus as the Bridegroom obtains His bride who are the overcomers of the church; but in *Eternity* His bride will be the result of the consummation or the

The Key to "Revelation"

gathering up together of all His work from the beginning to the very end. All will be consummated in new Jerusalem and it will be Christ's eternal bride. The clue for me to this is to be found in the gates and the foundations of new Jerusalem. Let us therefore take note, first of all, that new Jerusalem has twelve gates inscribed with the names of the twelve tribes of Israel (Revelation 21:12). Thus signifying—to me, at least—that all which God will have done to Israel shall be consummated in this new Jerusalem. And second of all, let us take note that all which God will have done in the church shall also be consummated in new Jerusalem, because we are told that the names inscribed on the twelve foundations are those of the twelve apostles of the Lamb (v. 14). So the day is coming in Eternity when all the redeeming work of the Lord Jesus and of God will have been gathered up together and become the eternal bride of the eternal Bridegroom.

In Eternity it is all to be summed up in Christ Jesus, and the glory is the eternal glory of God. No wonder that twice, John, who knew the Lord Jesus so well, when he saw the two visions of the bride that had made herself ready and of the descending new Jerusalem and had heard what was yet to be done, lost his mind: he bowed down to the angel who had shared these things with him and worshiped him because all was so beautiful, good, wonderful, and glorious. He was completely overcome by it all and so he forgot himself. The angel had to correct him twice, and on each occasion said: "Don't worship me; I am only a fellow bondman of yours and of all those brethren who keep the words of this book and have the testimony of Jesus. Therefore, worship God" (see 19:10b-d and 22:9). For, significantly added the angel on the first occasion: "the spirit of prophecy is the testimony of Jesus" (again, 19:10e).

I asked myself this morning, When I see Christ in the kingdom and in Eternity and all that He has done, will I be so surprised, so overwhelmed that I—like John—will forget myself? Will that be my reaction? And will that be your reaction? Oh, the Lamb, slain from the foundation of the world, is eternally the Lamb. We see God and the Lamb on the throne, and His servants shall serve Him throughout the Ages of Ages, and they shall continually see His face. Amazing! Praise the Lord! Amen!

Part Two
The Testimony of Jesus:
in Relation to the Church

Chapter One

The Testimony of Jesus

Revelation of Jesus Christ, which God gave to him, to shew to his bondmen what must shortly take place; and he signified it, sending by his angel, to his bondman John, who testified the word of God, and the testimony of Jesus Christ, all things that he saw. Blessed is he that reads, and they that hear the words of the prophecy, and keep the things written in it; for the time is near.

I John, your brother and fellow-partaker in the tribulation and kingdom and patience, in Jesus, was in the island called Patmos, for the word of God, and for the testimony of Jesus.

Revelation 1:1-3, 9

And when it opened the fifth seal, I saw underneath the altar the souls of them that had been slain for the word of God, and for the testimony which they held.

Revelation 6:9

And they have overcome him by reason of the blood of the Lamb, and by reason of the word of their testimony, and have not loved their life even unto death.

And the dragon was angry with the woman, and went to make war with the remnant of her seed, who keep the commandments of God, and have the testimony of Jesus.

Revelation 12:11, 17

And I fell before his feet to do him homage. And he says to me, See thou do it not. I am thy fellow-bondman, and the fellow-bondman of thy brethren who have the testimony of Jesus. Do homage to God. For the spirit of prophecy is the testimony of Jesus.

Revelation 19:10

I believe that upon our having read together these various fragments from the book of Revelation you will know what the subject is which we are going to consider this morning. The key verse for our consideration today and, God willing, perhaps for other times to come will be Revelation 19:10e—"the spirit of prophecy is the testimony of Jesus."

Now we all know this book of Revelation is a book of prophecy, for it states clearly at its very beginning that it is "the revelation of Jesus Christ which God gave him to show to his servants what must shortly take place." And it is further stated: "Blessed is he that reads, and they that hear the words of the prophecy, and keep the things written in it."

The nature of this book is therefore prophetic, and Biblical prophecy includes in its meaning two different characteristics. Ordinarily we think of prophecy as foretelling something that has not yet come to pass. Prophecy does include this element: to foretell what is to come. Even so, prophecy in the Bible not only includes *fore*telling but also "*forth*telling." To "forthtell" is to tell whoever it may be what the mind of God is.

So from reading the whole Bible we may conclude that some statements or passages in the Bible do contain prophecy since they may be foretelling a coming event of some kind. That is in fact quite true, but if we know the meaning of prophecy well enough, we will understand that the entire Bible is a volume of prophecy in the latter's two primary characteristics: sometimes the Bible is engaged in foretelling and sometimes, in "forthtelling": sometimes it is telling its readers what is to come and at other times it is telling them what the mind of God is. And hence, whether foretelling or "forthtelling," Revelation is a book laden to the full with prophecy.

All Biblical prophecy, of course, is given by God. It is not something uttered by the will of man but by holy men of old who, having been filled by the Holy Spirit, spoke forth the things of God (II Peter 1:21). They were simply speaking forth the mind of God. Therefore, we cannot interpret any prophecy according to our personal fancy or idea. We must be very careful when we attempt to understand what has been prophesied. For what may occur is that the more we may delve into prophecies the more we may become buried in the immense number of them, leading us gradually, unknowingly, or unconsciously to develop a particular system of interpretation, resulting in our becoming a self-appointed prophet. Instead of remaining students of prophecy we have become teachers of prophecy. And that can be a very dangerous development, in that we could end up being very dogmatic and dead sure of our particular set of interpretations. Moreover, we might even ultimately begin treating our interpretations as being Scripture itself and that if others did not agree with them, we might end up accusing them of not even believing the Bible.

Now I happened to have encountered this very type of person when I was in Peru on one occasion. There was an elderly Christian, a servant of the Lord there, and we were talking together. He held a different interpretation from mine. Nevertheless, I told him that I was open to considering others' interpretation and told him that though this or that was the viewpoint I currently held to regarding various prophecies, I was open to correction. Even so, that brother adhered to such a firm position on his interpretation that he ended up accusing me of not believing the Bible. I told him that I believed the word of God, that every part of God's word was true, but so far as the matter of interpretation is concerned, we believers may not always interpret correctly.

So on the one hand, I think it can be a most interesting and fascinating endeavor to study the prophecies in the Bible; on the other hand, when studying prophecies, we ought to be careful not to be dogmatic. Let us not be too sure of our interpretation but always remain open to the Lord for His light.

Furthermore, we can become so bogged down in our study of the words of prophecy that we may in the end merely touch the *letter* and actually overlook the *spirit* of prophecy. Having said that, however, I do not wish to imply that we can at all neglect the letter of the word of God. No, not in the least, for all the words in Scripture are spiritual and there is therefore the need of a work by the Spirit to enlighten us regarding the spirit of prophecy. Which is to say that, yes, we must hold fast the letter of prophecy because otherwise, we lack the ground or basis upon which the Spirit can build in His work of enlightening us; and yet, merely adhering to the letter of prophecy will kill us (cf. II Corinthians 3:6b): it is the Spirit that quickens and gives life (John 6:63a).

So my concern is that I not lead any of us into merely considering or pointing to the letter of prophecy. Perhaps on another occasion when there is more time, I would like very much to lead us into a detailed study of prophecy in terms of prophecy's letters because such a study would be truly fascinating. However, to me there is something much more important than the letter of prophecy and that is its spirit. So my aim today is not for us to focus on the words or letter of Biblical prophecy, though I truly believe every letter and every word of it; but my aim during these days is for us to focus our attention upon the spirit that lies behind the letter or words of prophecy.

The Testimony of Jesus

You may have read the book of Revelation many times. I have met many Christians who have never once read it. In fact, they were even told they should not touch the book because it was too difficult to read and understand. And yet we find at the very beginning of this book the following words of instruction: "he that reads and they that hear"—which is to say, that this book is for someone to read aloud and for the audience—a congregation, if you will—that gathers together, to listen to its text. Moreover, he that reads and they that hear shall be blessed for doing so (Revelation 1:3).

Now in my supposing you have read the book of Revelation, I will go a step further and suppose that you have spent some time in God's word studying its words of prophecy. Perhaps you are able to list out all the Bible's prophecies according to their order. And perhaps you are even able to join history and prophecy together and to assert: "This foretold event is the fulfillment of this or that prophecy." I do not know how many are able to do such a thing but I will grant that some of you are able to do it. Even if you can, however, can you tell me what the spirit is of this or that prophetic word? You may have asserted, for example, that a particular foretold earthquake event is the fulfillment of a certain prophetic verse in the Bible, but can you tell me what the spirit of that prophecy is? What my concern is is simply this: that though we may be able to know and keep the prophetic words right down to the very last letter, and yet we may miss the very spirit of it all.

Let us recall the story of the rich young ruler (Mark 10:17-22) who ran up to the Lord Jesus and knelt down before Him in the midst of a crowd surrounding him. Bear in mind those descriptive words: young, rich, ruler. He was not afraid to run. He was not afraid to kneel before the Lord in the presence of all those people. He was not hesitant to ask for help: What must I do that I may inherit eternal life?—thus indicating he knew the importance of eternal life: without eternal life nothing else mattered: he greatly desired to inherit eternal life. And Jesus looked upon him with love (Mark 10:21). The Lord replied, "Keep the commandments." The young man was surprised, even shocked, that Jesus had nothing new to offer but "to honor one's father and mother, to not commit adultery, steal, or bear false witness," and so forth. And this rich young ruler looked at the Master and said, "I have kept all these from my childhood." It is as though he were asking the Lord, "What more? What must I do?" Oh, how much the Lord loved that young man, a fact one could clearly see! Jesus in response continued to look at him with deep love and said, "If you want to be perfect, go and give to the poor, and come, follow Me." When that rich young man heard this response from the Master, he went home deeply sad, for he had faithfully kept all the *letters* of the Law but had violated the *spirit* of the Law. Outwardly he honored his parents, outwardly he did not steal, outwardly he did not bear false witness, and so forth; yet inwardly, he lacked love for his needy neighbors.

Now we know that the Ten Commandments had been inscribed by the finger of Jehovah God on two tablets of stone (Deuteronomy 9:10a). The first tablet told of man's relationship with God; the second tablet, of man's relationship with his fellowmen. Now the spirit which lay behind the first tablet's set of commandments was this: "to love the Lord thy God with all thine heart." And the spirit of the second tablet's commandments was "to love thy neighbor as thyself." Nevertheless, this rich young man loved money more than his neighbor. He was not able to part with his money for the poor among his neighbors whether near or far. His problem was that he had been keeping the letter of the Law but violating its spirit: this young rich ruler was willing to part with his neighbor but not with his money. Are we—like this young man—guilty of keeping the letter of the commandments but breaking their very spirit?

Another incident to illustrate this matter was what the apostle Paul had been doing when previously he had been known as Saul. As a Pharisee according to the righteousness of the Law, he was perfect and totally blameless; and yet Saul could zealously go from house to house to search out those simple, sincere and honest Christians, arrest them and even have them murdered. So the point I am trying to make here is that to hold fast the letter of Christ is not enough; we most certainly must do that, yes, but added to that there must also be present the spirit of Christ.

At this point, perhaps we must ask the question, Exactly what is the spirit of Christ? Even more specifically, What is the spirit? We have alluded to it already. The spirit is that which lies behind the letter: the spirit inspires the letter: in fact, the spirit is what the letter points to. Is that clear? The spirit is the power behind the form of the letter; or to phrase it another way, the spirit is the eternal embedded in the temporal; or yet another way to explain the matter, the spirit is the life hidden in the letter. The letter, though necessary for understanding, is nonetheless incidental because the spirit is that which is heavenly. Accordingly, unless we discern the spirit of a thing we touch only the superficial. The outward appearance is superficial because it is temporal and therefore is not the important element. The spirit is what is behind the appearance, behind the temporal, behind the letter. Thus, the spirit is eternal and that is what is important. If we only touch the letter of something, we are being superficial. It is still our superficial life coming through and being expressed and brings us into bondage, but if we reach or touch the spirit, then we are at peace, for wheresoever the spirit is, there is liberty (cf. II Corinthians 3:17).

Hence, even in this matter of studying prophecy, it is not enough for us only to touch the letter of God's prophetic words, we must also—and more importantly—discern their spirit. So what is the spirit of prophecy? Here we have before us all these prophecies in the book of Revelation, but what is their spirit? I believe we have the answer clearly and succinctly explained in this book's chapter 19 and verse 10e: "the spirit of prophecy is the testimony of Jesus." Permit me to say that during these few days this sentence of Scripture has come back to me again and again: "the spirit of prophecy is the testimony of Jesus."

Now we have to break this sentence down further by inquiring: What is a testimony? We often use that term. In our conversation, in our praise, in our various written communications among ourselves, we often employ this word, testimony. What do we mean by it?

We perhaps recognize that in God's word this term is used in different ways to mean, indicate, or define different things. Let me say at the outset of our discussion together today on this matter of testimony that it is necessary for us to lay the ground for future consideration; and hence, we probably cannot proceed too far further without first consulting God's word and try to lay some foundation concerning this term testimony for better understanding what is to follow later.

Let us begin by turning to Exodus 16:34—"Jehovah had commanded Moses, so Aaron deposited it before the Testimony, to be kept." The Lord here commanded Moses, and Aaron departed and placed the manna in the golden pot before the testimony to be kept. We find here the phrase, before the testimony. What is that? Let us next turn to Exodus 30:6—"thou shalt put it in front of the veil which is before the ark of the testimony in front of the mercy-seat which is over the testimony, where I will meet with thee." God commanded Moses to put the golden oil of incense before the veil which is before the ark of the testimony. Here the ark is called the ark of the testimony that is situated in front of the mercy seat which in turn is located over the testimony. Let us be clear in understanding what this verse tells us: the ark is called here the ark of the testimony; and yet, elsewhere in Scripture the ark is itself often called the testimony. On the one hand, therefore, we read about the ark of testimony, and read, on the other hand, simply about the testimony. Let us recall that all the following

The Testimony of Jesus

things—the golden pot of manna, Aaron's rod that had budded, and the two tablets of the Law—were placed in front of the testimony; or we may say that they were placed within the ark of testimony. Here, then, is the first place in Scripture where the ark is called the testimony.

Let us turn to another Bible passage, this time in Exodus 25:16—"thou shalt put into the ark the testimony that I shall give thee." We have already noted that the ark is the testimony, but this passage tells us that God commanded Moses to put the testimony in the ark. Now what exactly is that testimony? Well, by reading other Bible passages we come to know that the testimony is the Law as represented by the two tablets of Law which we know of as the Ten Commandments. The Ten Commandments have also been called, or referred to as, the testimony. Yet this is not only true with respect to the Ten Commandments but with respect also to the whole Mosaic Law, it likewise being called, or referred to as, the testimony. As evidence of this, let us look at a few places in the Bible which will confirm this fact.

II Kings 11—It was at the time of this passage that Jehoiada, Judah's high priest, had made Joash that nation's king. And so we read the following in verse 12—"he brought forth the king's son [Joash], and put the crown upon him, and gave him the testimony; and they made him king, and anointed him; and they clapped their hands, and said, Long live the king." What constituted the testimony which was given the new king? It was not only the Ten Commandments but the entire Mosaic Law as well.

Another relevant Scripture passage is Psalm 78:5—"he established a testimony in Jacob, and appointed a law in Israel, which he commanded our fathers, that they should make them known to their children." We know that these two phrases—the testimony in Jacob and a law in Israel—are references to precisely the same thing. In other words, the testimony is the

Law which was given to Israel that it might be kept by the fathers and handed down to their children.

Another Scripture which can be mentioned is Isaiah 8:16—"Bind up the testimony, seal the law among my disciples." Again we see that both testimony and Law mean the same thing; and further, in verse 20 we find these two phrases—"to the law and [to] the testimony"—have reference once more to the same thing: the entire Law of Moses. The whole Mosaic Law with the Ten Commandments at its center is here referred to as the testimony.

Still another relevant passage of Scripture is Numbers 9:15—"On the day that the tabernacle was set up, the cloud covered the tabernacle of the tent of testimony, and at evening it was upon the tabernacle as appearance of fire, until the morning." Here we read that the tent or tabernacle is called the testimony. Many places in Exodus refer to the tabernacle as the tabernacle of the testimony. The Old Testament makes frequent mention not only of the testimony, as we see here, but also of the people of Israel as the people of the testimony; and this is because they had the testimony with them. We can cite and read a few Scripture passages for that as well. Psalm 81:5, for instance—"He ordained it in Joseph for a testimony when he went forth over the land of Egypt, where I heard a language that I knew not." And again in Psalm 132:12—"If thy children keep my covenant, and my testimonies which I will teach them, their children also for evermore shall sit upon thy throne."

From all these Old Testament Scriptures, therefore, we have come to see and understand a few points. First, the ark was called the testimony. Second, the Law was also called the testimony. Third, the Law of the testimony was put within the ark of the testimony. Fourth, the laws and statutes in the ark are placed inside the tent of testimony. And fifth, the people of God are called the people of the testimony.

So I would have us come back to my original question: What is the meaning of this Biblical term, testimony? I believe a few comments are in order, which I trust will be helpful to our understanding. First, a testimony is that which is based upon a reality. If you want to bear a testimony, you must know a fact. If there is no fact, how can you testify? The apostle John was able to testify. And why? Because he was shown and given a fact. Indeed, he was shown and given many facts. So, first of all, a testimony must be based upon reality. Without reality there can be no testimony. If, under *that* circumstance, you do give testimony, it all will be false.

Second, a testimony must be that which has been revealed. In other words, that reality—that fact—must have been revealed to you—that is, it must have been seen and heard by you. Now, how can you testify to something if you have not seen and heard it? Let us suppose that there is a fact which has been manifested but you were not there to apprehend it: you have neither seen it nor heard it. Can you go forth and testify concerning it? You cannot, because it has not been revealed to you. Hence, there must first be a reality and there must then be a revelation. Please note, in this regard, what is asserted at the very outset of the book of Revelation: in the first verse—"the Revelation of Jesus Christ"; and in the second verse—"the testimony of Jesus Christ."

The testimony of or concerning Jesus is based upon the revelation of Jesus. Because Jesus has been revealed, therefore, there is a testimony.

And the third of my comments is, that a testimony must be a report made. A testimony is that which is spoken forth and not kept hidden in one's heart. It is not enough for anyone to have only the first two points comprising what a testimony is. No, a person must likewise speak forth the word of testimony.

Accordingly, a testimony must include these three elements: First—Reality; second—Revelation; and, third—Report. If a Christian has these three elements, then that one has a testimony.

Then we come to this matter of the ark. What, from the Scripture, can we say about the ark? The ark was made of gold, that which was physical and material. The ark was therefore an outward-appearing object that could be seen although it remained hidden behind the tabernacle veil but which the high priest beheld once a year upon entering the most holy place.

Whereas God is invisible and the ark was not; nevertheless, whenever a person saw the ark he saw God. Indeed, wherever the ark was, there was the presence of God, for the ark was that which set forth God. Hence, because the ark revealed God and told the people about Him, therefore, in the Old Testament Scriptures the ark was called the testimony of the Law.

Nobody knows the mind of God, but the Mosaic Law has revealed His mind to a certain degree; and because of that, because, further, there is the reality behind the letter of the Law, and because, still further, the Law shows us what God desires and requires, the Law was called the testimony in the Old Testament.

Moreover, the tabernacle was called the tent of the testimony because it was the vessel or instrument which contained and held forth to the world the testimony concerning the one true God. But so were the people of God back then because they held the testimony, bore the testimony, and spoke out the testimony. In short, they lived for the testimony.

So what is the testimony for us who are the people of God today in the world? It is none other than the testimony concerning Jesus. We have noted already that the spirit of prophecy is the testimony concerning the Lord Jesus. And there is but one testimony in this universe: the testimony of Jesus. All the words of Biblical prophecy, and the spirit of all those words, have but one focus or center: it is called the testimony of Jesus.

All Biblical prophecy speaks of one person and only one. This is true whether one has in mind the book of Revelation or the whole Bible; but for the sake of our discussion today let us limit our consideration to just the book of Revelation. Oh, concerning this one Bible book, there are so many different interpretations. The book touches upon so many fascinating things: for instance, seven seals, seven trumpets, seven vials, seven thunderings. And then there are things in it which concern the church, the Gentiles, and the Jews. Moreover, this book speaks of things in heaven and on earth and underneath the earth, as well as references are made in it to the old creation and to the new; and it can be said, also, that this book's content is concerned with not only human beings but with living creatures, mountains, waters and lands, and even touches upon angels both good and bad. Undeniably, because there are so many interesting things in this book, one can easily lose oneself in its many wonders! Nevertheless, we need to ask ourselves, Why, really, does God touch upon all these things in its pages?—Why does He foretell and/or "forthtell" concerning all these various matters? Why? That we may know what the seven thunderings say or mean? No, you will probably never know or be able to discern that. Then why? For only one reason: for the testimony of Jesus, the One who is most precious to God the Father and to us believers in Jesus.

Permit me to say that if we see these wonders and fail to see the *Wonder* of wonders—even Jesus Christ, the Son of God—then we will miss the whole meaning of salvation and shall end up being barely saved. Oh, may we truly understand that the spirit of all the prophecies in the Bible is nothing but the testimony of Jesus. Oh, that we may see Him in all these wondrous things.

And therefore, I hope we have together laid a helpful foundation for our future consideration.

Chapter Two

The Vision of the Son of Man

I John, your brother and fellow-partaker in the tribulation and kingdom and patience, in Jesus, was in the island called Patmos, for the word of God, and for the testimony of Jesus. I became in the Spirit on the Lord's day, and I heard behind me a great voice as of a trumpet, saying, What thou seest write in a book, and send to the seven [churches]: to Ephesus, and to Smyrna, and to Pergamos, and to Thyatira, and to Sardis, and to Philadelphia, and to Laodicea.

And I turned back to see the voice which spoke with me; and having turned, I saw seven golden [lampstands], and in the midst of the seven [lampstands] one like the Son of man, clothed with a garment reaching to the feet, and girt about at the breasts with a golden girdle: his head and hair white like white wool, as snow; and his eyes as a flame of fire; and his feet like fine brass, as burning in a furnace; and his voice as the voice of many waters; and having in his right hand seven stars; and out of his mouth a sharp two-edged sword going forth; and his countenance as the sun shines in its power.

And when I saw him I fell at his feet as dead; and he laid his right hand upon me, saying, Fear not; I am the first and the last, and the living one: and I became dead, and behold, I am living to the ages of ages, and have the keys of death and of hades.

Revelation 1:9-18

The spirit of prophecy is the testimony of Jesus.

Revelation 19:10e

As was pointed out previously, the key verse in our ongoing consideration together of the book of Revelation is the fragment of Scripture in that book to be found at the end of 19:10: "the spirit of prophecy is the testimony of Jesus." It was mentioned last time that the book of Revelation is basically one of prophecy. God by His Spirit is found therein continually foretelling future events of all kinds. We sense today that even now we are living in the last days, for we see many of these events coming to pass very rapidly, and there are other events which are yet to come. So it will be a very profitable undertaking for us to read and meditate upon this book of Revelation and to be watchful as we wait to see how these events of prophecy will come to pass.

Even so, we are not to be concerned primarily with the letter—with the details—of these prophecies but to be concerned chiefly with the spirit of prophecy. Which is to say, that all these foretold events which have come and which are still to come have in them a real and significant meaning, and that significant meaning, we learned last time, is the spirit of prophecy—that which lies behind these prophetic events. In other words, the spirit of prophecy is what or who all these events point to—even to Jesus Christ. So our chief concern should always be the spirit, and not the letter or words, of prophecy. And the spirit of prophecy is the testimony concerning Jesus.

The Vision of the Son of Man

We have come to see, then, that God is chiefly interested in His Son Jesus Christ. Indeed, the primary reason He is interested in all the people, things, and events prophesied about in Revelation is because they all are related in one way or another to His Son. If they are not related to His Son, they have neither meaning nor purpose. If, therefore, you yourself are not related to Jesus Christ, permit me to say that God is not interested in you. Permit me to say further that your very life is meaningless—not only meaningless to God but meaningless and purposeless to yourself. Everything is related to God's Son Jesus Christ and it is only in *that* relatedness that you will ever find meaning and purpose in life. So if we can see the Lord Jesus as we delve into, study, and ponder all of Revelation's foretold things and events, then we have apprehended the spirit of prophecy, indeed!

Now in our time together today it is my desire that we may see and understand the testimony of Jesus in relation to His church, because that is what is to be found in the first three chapters of Revelation. Actually, however, this is not only to be found in the first three chapters but also throughout this entire book and which is consummated in its last two chapters.

Why is it that in Revelation the testimony of Jesus is first of all related to the church of God? I think the reason is very simple. It is because the church is the depository of the testimony of Jesus. God puts the testimony of Jesus into the church, which thus signifies that the church is the keeper and guardian of the testimony of Jesus, and, further, that the church is the instrument in God's hands for the proclaiming of the testimony of Jesus.

We will recall the history of the Israelites. The ark of the testimony was given to the people of Israel and thus they were to keep the ark. In one sense they were to guard and protect the ark but in another sense the ark was to protect them. So God gave the ark of His testimony to the people of Israel and they were to keep and guard it, yet they lost the ark. If the Law which

God gave them was lost to them, what was bound to happen? They would become a people with no purpose and no meaning. Sadly, that is what happened to the Israelites. In fact, they became worse than the Gentiles who had never had the Law of God—who had never had the ark of the testimony. But whenever, in Israel's ancient history, the ark of the testimony remained with them, whenever the Law of God was honored in their midst, they were blessed by God and they became the first of all the nations round about—they were the head and not the tail—which made such a difference.

Now the history of the church is just like that of the people of Israel. Permit me to say, however, that the church, and not Israel, has always been God's first love. It is quite true, of course, that time-wise Israel had appeared long before the church. Nevertheless, God's mind and heart was fixed upon the church from even before the foundation of the world. So it is the church of God today that has the testimony of Jesus. And having placed the testimony of Jesus in the church, God expects the church to keep and guard it but also to testify, spread abroad, and speak it forth. The church is therefore both the depository vessel of the testimony as well as the testifying instrument of the testimony. Hence, that is the reason we find in the book of Revelation that the testimony of Jesus is first spoken of in relation to the church.

Now if the church loses the testimony of Jesus and fails to testify concerning Him, will there be any meaning to the church? Will there be any reason for its existence? Let us inquire further that if the church can be seen by the world as constituting a great religious system with much tradition, many activities, and many good works but loses the testimony of Jesus by failing to spread the testimony of Jesus abroad, then in God's eyes she is nothing and means nothing to Him and has nothing to do with His economy, plan, or purpose. That is why, according to Revelation's first three chapters, if a church failed to keep the testimony of Jesus, the lampstand was to be removed

(Revelation 2:5). In other words, she is no longer considered by God to be a church because she failed in her function and mission.

We can therefore appreciate the seriousness of this matter. The testimony of Jesus is that which truly matters to God. It has been entrusted to the church for her to keep it faithfully and to testify abroad concerning Jesus. If a church fails in this she is a total failure. Let us be aware that God is not deceived by anything extraordinary nor by anything less than what He wants. He knows what He is after, and it is only what He is after that can satisfy Him and nothing else. Oh, may the Lord arrest us with the same desire so that we may not in any way be satisfied with merely outward activities, many good works, great tradition, or with even a very great system; for if we do not have the testimony of Jesus with us, if in fact the glory of the Lord has departed (cf. Revelation 2:19-20, I Samuel 4:21-22), then what is the meaning of what is today's counterpart to the temple of old? It has no meaning and is therefore nothing.

Let me put this matter another way. If the people of the world should come into contact with the church of God they should be able to see Jesus, hear Jesus and be able to be in touch with Jesus. And hopefully, some of them, having been deeply attracted to Jesus through the church's testimony, may even become enraptured by Him. In short, the people of God are not to testify of themselves but to bear the testimony of only one person and that is the Lord Jesus.

Permit me further to say the following concerning this very serious matter. Suppose people should come to the church gathering and all they see, hear and come into contact with are only the people there. Those outside visitors might even say, "Well, the people in the church are nice people, for when we arrived and sat down, they were all so nice to us. Moreover, they all looked nice themselves." Those visitors might even have commented later: "Oh, we met some very nice people in that church."

The Key to "Revelation"

Or suppose people from outside come in contact with the church and hear things concerning politics, people from other lands, liberty, freedom, perhaps even the expression of philosophical thoughts—all no doubt very good things. Nevertheless, if that is all they have heard, if that is the only impression they take with them as they depart the church meeting, they have visited the wrong place because they have not seen or heard Jesus, since the church is for the testimony of Jesus and nothing else. All that people should see and hear and touch and be filled with in the church of God should be Jesus and not anyone or anything else. The testimony of Jesus has been entrusted to the church today and she is therefore to bear only that testimony alone.

But a most important question arises, which is, How can we bear the testimony concerning Jesus if we ourselves have not seen Him, if we ourselves have not heard Him, if we ourselves do not know Him? How absolutely essential it is that we who are the Lord's people should know Him. We should see Him, hear Him, and be filled by Him so that our testimony to the world concerning Jesus may be living and strong. It is not only our duty and responsibility but it is our privilege to make Him known through the church.

So we find that at the beginning of Revelation the testimony of Jesus is first of all related to His church. John was exiled to the Isle of Patmos in the Aegean Sea. The apostle himself has informed the reader that he was exiled there for the word of God and for the testimony of Jesus and that on a certain Lord's day, just as on a given Lord's day today, he was in the Spirit and heard behind him a voice like a trumpet that instructed him to write in a book what he saw and send it to seven identified assemblies or churches situated in Asia Minor. When John heard this voice, he turned around to see that voice and beheld a wondrous vision.

Now what did John see? One of the elements in the vision which he saw were seven golden lampstands. These lampstands

The Vision of the Son of Man

or candlesticks upon which would sit lamps to shed light were literally lampstands and not lamps. So John reported that he saw seven golden lampstands, and in the midst of them he beheld one like the Son of man. Now that was the vision, and as we consider this vision together let us bear in mind that this is the testimony of Jesus to which John was testifying. What, then, is the meaning of these seven golden lampstands which John saw? The Son of man—even the Lord Jesus Christ—explained to John that the seven lampstands he had seen were those same seven churches or assemblies in Asia Minor which had already been identified by name and that were to receive the book John was instructed to write and send out. And hence, these lampstands represented those seven Asian churches.

In one very important sense the church is one. There is but one church of Christ. All who belong to the Lord, all who are redeemed by His blood and are born again of the Holy Spirit, are members of the one body of Christ that comprise the universal church of God (I Corinthians 12:12-13). In another sense, however, and because we Christians are still living in our physical bodies and are thus restricted by time and space, there is the necessity for there to be church assemblies in different places throughout the world. If, therefore, I am here in New York, I cannot be in Washington; and if I am in Washington, I cannot be in New York. Hence, because of believers being limited by time and space, these various church assemblies—whether they be located in Asia Minor or elsewhere in the world—have, nonetheless, a direct link or relationship to the one universal church of God.

Now let us be very clear that these seven lampstands—which represented the already identified seven churches in Asia Minor and in a sense are representative of all the churches of God throughout the world—formed the background of the vision which John saw; and the one like the Son of man whom John saw in the midst of the lampstands formed or served as the foreground. John's vision was thus the following: the seven

Asian churches served as the background and Christ was the foreground. We will never be able to explain Christ without the background of the church. On the other hand, we can never explain the church if we do not see Christ. This is because Christ is the Head and the church is His body. Which means that we cannot explain the Head if we do not touch the body. Conversely, how can anyone understand the body if there is no Head? Therefore, we see in John's vision that the church forms the background and the Son of man forms the foreground.

We may even explain the matter another way, as follows. What we see in this Patmos vision is what Scripture refers to as the "new man" (Ephesians 2:15). The Head is the glorified Son of man who, of course, is Christ. He is seen at this vision's center—the foreground—and His body is the church—the vision's background—which is the expression of Christ's fullness and richness. And they together, Head and body, are united into one. We may therefore conclude that what the Lord Jesus as Head is to the body—which is His people, His church—is *everything*. And, consequently, what the Lord Jesus' relationship to His church today is as the Son over His house (Hebrews 3:6a), the Head over the body of Christ. And because of that fact, what the Head is, the body ought to be. If there be any discrepancy, contradiction, or difference between the Head and His body, then the testimony of Jesus will be adversely affected. On the other hand, if the body is what the Head is, the result will be that the testimony is full and strong.

What, therefore, is the church? She is the fullness of Him who fills all in all (Ephesians 1:23). She is the expression of the riches of the Head. In fact, what the Head is is what is to be manifested through the body. And that is what the church is. Are we such? Is that our testimony? Do we give people the impression that the Lord Jesus is rich and strong, or do we leave them with the impression that He is quite poor and weak? —or, even as some theologians have pronounced, that God—the Son of God—is dead? What exactly is the impression we give to the world?

A further point I wish to make here is this: that we cannot emphasize the church to the extent of losing sight of Christ because the church is not at all the center of everything. The center of our sight is, and must always be, Christ. Even though the church is indeed only the background, nevertheless, we need that background; for if we do not have that, we will not be able to see Christ. Now some of us might say: "Well, I do in fact see Christ without the aid of the church, for I see Him as my Savior. Once I was in sin and transgressions. Once I was under the burden and load of sin. Once I cried alone and as I was struggling in my sin the Lord revealed himself to me, He showed me how He had died on the cross for me and when I trusted Him as my Savior I was saved. Have I not therefore seen and known Christ? Hence, I did not need the church for me to have come to know Christ." But I would sincerely say in response: How much of Him do you really know?

I am reminded here of what Paul had prayed, as recorded in chapter 3 of his Ephesian letter: "Oh, that we may grasp how wide and long and high and deep is the love of Christ that exceeds knowledge so that we may be filled with all the fullness of God." Yet how are we to grasp and know the fullness of God that is in Christ? Paul's explanation was this: "with all the saints." You and I alone can only know Christ to a certain degree, and by comparison it will generally be very little. We need the church by which to know the fullness of God in Christ (see vv. 17b-19). The Lord Jesus is so great and so full and so rich that it is not possible for any one of us to know Him in fullness, and it therefore requires the entire church to know Him fully.

If you are in fellowship with the saints, you are in a position to know the Lord in His fullness. If, though, you seek Christ all by yourself, you thinking you alone are able to know Him, then your vision of Christ will be very limited and small. Scripture thus makes clear that we need the church, which in John's vision served as the necessary background: without the background we can never see and apprehend Christ in all His glory; without the church we cannot comprehend Him in His fullness. That is undeniably a true statement. In order to see the Lord, therefore, we need the church as the background, and in order to know the church we must see the Lord as the foreground. The two must go together.

The trouble with many Christians today is that some want the Lord but do not want the church whereas others want the church but do not want the Lord. That is impossible. Such positions are nothing but earthly mirages; they can never serve as the content of a heavenly vision. What John's heavenly vision consisted of was the glorified Son of man standing in the midst of the churches—the Lord of glory being the foreground and the churches, the background. It is necessary for both to be seen together.

There is always the danger, of course, of our becoming so involved with the church that we may lose sight of Christ, who is the center. The vision which was given John to see is of Christ as the foreground and the church as the background. The church is a lampstand whose responsibility is to lift up Christ as light and life; and thus John beheld the Son of man—even Christ the Lord—standing in the midst of the seven golden lampstands.

Now because we find the seven churches here and find Christ in their midst, therefore, we can conclude that the vision is the testimony concerning Jesus in relation to His church. But what is the content of that testimony? The Spirit of God revealed to the apostle John a total of ten different descriptions of Christ as the glorified Son of man to help us understand what is the testimony about Jesus in relation to His church.

First, the relevant passage reads that in the midst of the lampstands there was one like the Son of man. This is most unusual. If we were to write this passage we would most likely state that there stood in the midst of the seven lampstands one

The Vision of the Son of Man

like the Son of *God*. That would seem more reasonable than to describe that figure as one whose appearance was like the Son of man.

In contemplating this vision, immediately our minds will most likely recall the prophecy of Daniel. Daniel the prophet, you may remember, lived during the time of the Babylonian captivity. He himself was captured and brought to Babylon and was eventually made one of the prime ministers there. Chapter 7 of Daniel's book tells of his having seen a vision on one occasion, and in that vision he beheld the last days of world history when God, whose throne Daniel saw set up, would judge all the nations. The prophet witnessed in the vision millions of angels in attendance at that throne and God, the Ancient of Days, seated thereon. Daniel then saw someone being led to the throne, and to this one was given dominion and power and glory and kingdom, and who would judge all the nations; and this one whom Daniel beheld in the vision was described by the prophet as having the appearance like that of the Son of man. God is here seen giving the judgment of all the earth's nations to one like unto the Son of man.

Yet here in John's vision this same Son of man is not shown as one who is judging the *nations* but one who is seen dispensing judgment upon the church. Yes, there is coming a day that Christ as the Son of man shall indeed judge all the nations, but today He, as the Son of man, is engaged in judging the church, the house of God. There is much more which could be said about this, but I think this is enough for now.

We need to inquire as to the meaning of this title, "the Son of man." When Jesus was here on earth He often referred to himself as the Son of man. Whereas Jesus is undeniably the Son of God, His favorite way of referring to himself was the Son of man. Basically this title of Jesus' as the Son of man has two meanings surrounding it. First, it conveys the fact that Christ came to this earth as a man. Though He is God, He nonetheless came down to us from highest heaven and took upon himself the physical body of a created human being. In His thus becoming a man the Son of God nevertheless did so without ever relinquishing His deity. Though Jesus is in fact God, He is a man—a *real* man—a human being like you and me. The Son of God took upon himself flesh, thus identifying himself with mankind in order that we may be identified with Him in His resurrection and in His glory.

Hence, first of all, it can be said that this title, Son of man, tells us that Jesus the Son of God is truly also a man. He is a man who knows our frailties—who has been tempted in all things, sin excepted—who can sympathize with us—in short, a man who knows us because He is one of us. On the other hand, we may sometimes look upon Jesus as being only God. And naturally, if He is God He can easily do this and He can readily do that. And why? Because He is God, and because of that fact, there is no frailty, weakness, imperfection or limitation with Him. All of that is quite true about Jesus in His deity; but we are human beings with weaknesses and imperfections and limitations of every sort. Consequently, the Son of God, in order that He might enter into sympathy with us, became a man—a perfect man.

But the title, the Son of man, conveys a second meaning or thought: Christ the Son of God is not only a man, He is also *the* man—the man of God's choice—the man of God's purpose—the man whom God had in mind when he created Adam. Adam, of course, fell; but in Christ, God has finally gotten His man of choice. Christ as the Son of man is the man after whose order we were created and are destined to become. We may therefore say, secondly, that this title means that Christ Jesus as the Son of man is the beginning of a new race. As the Son of man Christ Jesus began a new order of mankind: a mankind after His order and not after the old order of Adam, the head of fallen mankind. What the Son of man is so shall we be because He will make us to be one that we may become conformed to His image

The Vision of the Son of Man

(Romans 8:29a). Now that is the all-encompassing meaning of that title, the Son of man.

The Lord Jesus today is *the* one. Once He was on this earth in humiliation. He was despised, rejected, and crucified because of His apparent weakness; today, however, He is ascended. Before Jesus' ascension back to the Father there was no man in heaven at the right hand of God. Indeed, no man was able to enter into the presence of God; for because of his sin, man was barred from God's presence and barred from dwelling with God (cf. Genesis 3:23). But thank God, Jesus was raised from the dead, and He ascended up on high in returning to His Father. Yet, in returning, the risen and ascended Lord Jesus did so not only as the eternal Son but also as the Son of man.

Oh, how we can rejoice that there is now a Man in heaven, there is a Man on the throne, there is a Man at the right hand of God the Father. Moreover, let us not forget that that Man continually acts there for us in His intercessory ministry. When Stephen was stoned to death he saw the Son of man standing (and not, in this instance, sitting) at the right hand of God (Acts 7:56). That is our Benefactor, even Jesus, the Son of man. Is that not immensely wonderful? The Man whom Paul met on the way to Damascus said to him: "I am Jesus whom you persecute" (Acts 9:5b). But bear in mind that He is no longer a man of humiliation. He is now *the* Man in glory.

Let us realize afresh that the Lord Jesus as the Son of man is in glory, and because He is in glory He will lead many sons into glory (Hebrews 2:10a). Oh what a blessed hope is ours! How can we be assured of our acceptance by God? How can we be sure that one day we will be there with God forever? Because there is *the* Man there. He is our guarantee; for He is our pledge, our Savior, our Intercessor, and our High Priest; and He is there in order to bring *us* there, too. He is there as the Man of Glory and He will bring us men and women there.

So we find here in John's vision the Lord Jesus standing as one who is like the Son of man. His relationship with the church today is, in fact, as a son over God's house (Hebrews 3:6a).

The vision shown John and described in the first chapter of Revelation is a vision of the Son over His house. Here the risen and ascended Lord Jesus is presented as both the Son of man and the Son of God. He is, as it were, looking over His house and taking care of His house. In fact, He is putting His house in order, in that, He is making His house a perfect reflection of what He himself is. And because of that, there is judgment involved; there is also encouragement and exhortation involved; there is both sympathy and help involved as well. In summary, it is the Son exercising His responsibility over His house. What house is it? It is the holy house of God, and it is the boast of the Lord.

What, then, is the testimony concerning Jesus today? What is the content of the testimony that has been entrusted to us as the church today? Is it not one like the Son of man who is the Son over His house? He is there among the assemblies of the church seeking and working to transform and conform His people to His image and ultimately to bring His many sons to glory (Romans 12:2b, 8:29a, Hebrews 2:10a). Now that is the testimony of Jesus in relation to His house—even the church which is His body.

Well, now, that was the first description: one like the Son of man.

The second description of Christ the Son of man was: "clothed with a garment reaching to the feet." Garment in the Scriptures always stands for righteousness; which is therefore to say that here we behold the Lord as the righteous one. It is not only that Christ possesses *some* righteousness or has accomplished *some* righteous acts but that He is *the* Righteous One. Christ Jesus is seen here covered with a garment extending even down to His feet. Perhaps we are reminded of that verse in I John chapter 2: that if anyone sins, we have with the Father

The Vision of the Son of Man

an advocate, a patron, who speaks to the Father in our defense—even Jesus Christ the Righteous who is at the right hand of God and who is the propitiation for our sins—yet not only for ours but also for the sins of the entire world (see vv. 1b-2). Jesus Christ the Righteous One is our Intercessor, Comforter, and Advocate. He is the propitiation. If we fail, He never fails, because He is the propitiation—the atoning sacrifice—for our sins that satisfies God the Father.

The Son of man is described a third way: "[He was] gird about at the breast with the golden girdle." In Eastern countries people usually place a girdle around their garment because of the long garments they wear, and because of that, it is not very easy when anyone starts to work: the garment must therefore be girded up at one's waist in order to be able to work. But the girdle seen here is not around the waist but around the breast or chest area. From this it can be assumed that the emphasis of this third description is being placed not on work but on the center of one's affections which is the breast area. Now if a person possesses even just a little righteousness, that one will tend to be hard, harsh, and critical of others. He will measure or evaluate others according to his limited standards of righteousness, and if they do not meet even his miniscule standards, he will more than likely look down upon them. Is that not a picture of what we ourselves are? Yet described here is the Lord Jesus who is the totally and only Righteous One on earth, and yet he is not in any sense harsh or critical of others, for He is girded with a golden girdle around the center of His affections. In other words, though the Son of man is verily the Righteous One, He does not despise or reject others who fail and sin; rather, He is full of divine love—a love whose purpose is not to condone anyone's sin but to bring that one back to God.

Here is the fourth description of the Son of man: "His head and hair [were] white like white wool, as snow." Gray hair is the glory of man's head, in that it represents wisdom. And the hair of the Man in the vision was as white as white wool and snow. This betokens the fact that the Son of man is the fountain of wisdom to us. Indeed, He is wisdom to His church and doing everything according to His wisdom. And His wisdom is inexhaustible.

The fifth description: "his eyes [were] as a flame of fire." His eyes penetrate; they discern, consume, and purify. Whatever does not measure up to His uncompromising standard shall be consumed, but anything that is of Him shall be purified like gold. Such is the power of the Son of man's eyes! Peter met those penetrating eyes of His. While the disciple was at his weakest, failing moment—that of denying his Master three times—the Lord Jesus turned around while still on trial and looked straight at him (Luke 22:61). Oh, His eyes are like a flame of fire. They burn away the dross and purify the heart.

Here is the next description: "his feet [were] like fine brass, as burning in a furnace." The Son of man has trod the way of the cross and His legacy to us is a new and living way that we can follow from the cross.

Description number seven: "his voice [was] as the voice of many waters." Can we fail to hear his voice? I can still recall the very first time I came near to the sea but before I had arrived at the beach. Though at that point I was still quite far from the beach, I could hear the roaring voice of the sea's many waters and I could not bear it. Did not Jesus say, "My sheep hear My voice"? (John 10:27a) Can we hear His voice? Or are we so deaf that we cannot hear Him whose voice is like that of many waters?

Here is the eighth description: "and having in his right hand seven stars." We know that the seven stars are the angels of the previously identified seven Asia Minor churches, because this was what the Son of man himself told His disciple John. Let me add here by saying that these angels represent the spiritually responsible brothers and sisters in the churches. They, like the angels, are at the right hand of God with the Lord sustaining them with His power.

The next-to-the-last description is worded thus: "and out of his mouth [was] a sharp two-edged sword going forth." One day that sharp two-edged sword shall slay all of Jesus' enemies. This we read about in Revelation chapter 19, but here this word is related to the church. This description reminds us, does it not, what Hebrews 4:12 declares: God's word, sharper than any two-edged sword, is able to penetrate even to the dividing of the soul and the spirit and is able to discern the thoughts and intents of the heart.

And the final description is as follows: "and his countenance [was] as the sun shines in its power." We are aware, are we not, that the countenance of a person usually expresses what is within whereas one's garment tells us what is without. Within the Son of man it is all glorious. His countenance is therefore our help, our salvation, our spiritual health.

So we have all these descriptions of the Son of man, the Lord Jesus Christ. Yet, let us not be occupied with all these descriptive words of Him but let us be occupied with Him himself. In this wonderful vision He is in glory. He is so powerful and yet He is so gentle. He is so discerning, consuming and purifying, and yet, He is able to help. He is yearning for His own and yet He is intent on bringing His own to himself. In His essence the Son of man is all these things for us. So may God open our understanding and our hearts that shall allow Him to give us a vision of the glorified Son of man that will then constitute our testimony concerning Him.

John the beloved disciple, who saw this wonderful vision, now fell down as though dead at the feet of Jesus because He was so glorious. If we truly have a vision of the testimony of Jesus in relation to his church, our only reaction—like that of John—will be to fall at Jesus' feet as though dead.

Chapter Three

The Meaning of the Vision

And I turned back to see the voice which spoke with me; and having turned, I saw seven golden [lampstands], and in the midst of the seven [lampstands] one like the Son of man, clothed with a garment reaching to the feet, and girt about at the breasts with a golden girdle: his head and hair white like white wool, as snow; and his eyes as a flame of fire; and his feet like fine brass, as burning in a furnace; and his voice as the voice of many waters; and having in his right hand seven stars; and out of his mouth a sharp two-edged sword going forth; and his countenance as the sun shines in its power. And when I saw him I fell at his feet as dead; and he laid his right hand upon me, saying, Fear not; I am the first and the last, and the living one: and I became dead, and behold, I am living to the ages of ages, and have the keys of death and of hades. Write therefore what thou hast seen, and the things that are, and the things that are about to be after these.

Revelation 1:12-19

The following question was put to us at our previous gathering, and today I would place it here before us again: Have we caught the vision of the glorious Christ in His church? If we have caught that vision, there will not be and cannot be any room for us to boast. The only reaction for us to have is to fall down to the ground—as did John—as though dead. Having himself been raised from the dead, the risen Lord could touch

The Key to "Revelation"

His disciple and by that touch John was raised as from the dead. Thus was he strengthened by the Lord so that he could receive and enter into the message which God wanted to give him. And this is what I hope the Lord will do this morning as we consider further this vision of the glorious Son of man.

Now exactly what is the meaning of that glorious vision of the Son of man to His own? We need not try to figure it out because the glorious Lord himself told John (and to us, by extension) what the interpretation of that vision is. We will find that John saw a vision of the risen, ascended Lord in relation to His church and then John heard Him explain to him the meaning of what he had just then seen. And it was simply this. Read again what the glorified Son of man said to John: "Fear not; I am the first and the last, and the living one: and I became dead, and behold, I am living to the ages of ages, and have the keys of death and of hades." In this summary explanation of the Lord's regarding the tenfold description of himself as the glorified Head of the church, there are three distinct elements to it. First: I am the First and the Last; second: I am the Living One; and third: I became dead, and I am living forever and ever, and have the keys of death and of hades.

What is the Lord Jesus to us as His church? First, He is first and He is last, meaning that He is the All-Inclusive One, since if He is first and He is last, He is everything in between. Jesus is recorded elsewhere in Revelation as having made a similar statement of inclusiveness: "I am the alpha and the omega" (22:13a). The alpha is the first alphabet letter in the Greek language and the omega is its last letter. The English-language counterpart would be to say: I am the A and the Z. So, if the Lord is the A and the Z or the alpha and the omega, He is all the other letters of the alphabet in between as well. And thus the Lord Jesus is all that this or that alphabet can spell.

At the very beginning of our Christian experience we come to know the Lord Jesus as our personal Savior and that is great, but as we go on with Him we discover that He is not only our

The Meaning of the Vision

Savior but is also the One who is from A to Z to us. The risen, ascended Son of man is first and last, the beginning and end, the alpha and omega; and therefore, He has all that is in between and is the One who claims the right to spell out every detail and circumstance of our life. In other words, there is nothing in our life in which the Lord Jesus has no part; or, to put it another way, there is no part in our life in which He is not that part.

A concept similar to this was expressed by the apostle Paul in his Colossian letter's chapter 3. There Paul talks about that new man who is being renewed according to the image of Christ. He goes on to explain that in this new man—which is to say that in the church—there is neither Greek nor Jew, neither circumcision nor uncircumcision, no Barbarian or Scythian, neither bondman nor freeman; instead, Christ is everything and in everything (vv. 9b-11). What is Paul saying here? He is stating here that in the church there is, first of all, no Greek or Jew. The Jewish people had divided all the world into two kinds of people: Jews and Gentiles; nevertheless, asserts the apostle, in the church there is not to be either Jew or Gentile. Furthermore, Paul continued by declaring that besides there being neither Jew nor Gentile in this one new man that is the church, there is likewise not to be either circumcision or uncircumcision, barbarian or Scythian, bondman or freeman. But if that be the case, then we may naturally ask, Who will be there? And Paul's answer is quite simple: Only Christ is to be there; for, concludes the apostle, "He is all and in all." In other words, we may say that Christ, the Son of man, is the All-Inclusive One. In view of this, it may rightfully be asked: Do we know Jesus Christ as the All-Inclusive One? I shall be putting this probing question to ourselves as we continue in our discussion together today.

In response, we might be perplexed as to what is meant by that word all-inclusive. All right, I shall try to make it easier to understand by returning to each of the three elements comprising what the risen, ascended Son of man had said to His disciple John; His opening words being initially this: "I am the first." And in applying those four words to ourselves, we need to inquire: Is the Lord first in our affection? Is He first in our thinking? Does He have the first place in our lives? Whenever we begin to do anything, do we let Him begin it, or do we plan out everything and then simply ask Him to give His approval?—or do we let *Him* originate everything in our life? These are very practical questions to be asking ourselves.

How often we mistake or misinterpret the meaning of the word of God, in that, because Christ has also said, "I am the last," we therefore put Him last in our life. And so it ends up in our being first while letting Christ be last. That, of course, is not the meaning of the Son of man's word to John of His being the last, which will be explained later, but the opening point I wish to make here is that Christ is to be first in our life instead of it being the case that our business is our first interest or money is first or that our relationships have first place or that amusements take first place or that our own pleasure is elevated to first place, rather than that we put the Lord first. Do we see how practical Jesus' word to His disciple is? He clearly meant it when He declared: "I am [to be] ... first."

When confronted by this understanding of the Lord's word, we—as did John the beloved disciple—will fall down as though dead, for we know that we have not put Him first. In that same Colossian letter of Paul's, the apostle spoke in chapter 1 of the will of God (v. 9b). What is the eternal will of God? Simply this: that Christ may be first or have the supremacy in everything (v. 18c). Why must Christ be first and supreme in all things? Because all the fullness of the Godhead, explained Paul, dwells in Him bodily (v. 19). Christ Jesus is first because He is rich: He is rich in mercy, rich in grace, rich in righteousness, rich in love, rich in everything; and because He is so rich, therefore, He ought to be the first in everything having to do with all His disciples.

The Meaning of the Vision

Permit me to inquire: In the light of all which has been said, do you let Christ be first in your life? Indeed, this inquiry can be applied personally to all the different compartments, considerations, and circumstances of your life—in other words, everything in your life. Is Christ put first in your life? We often counsel ourselves or others to put first things first; however, we may sometimes say—in order to excuse ourselves—that it is very hard to know what *is* the first thing. Allow me to say, though, that for the Christian it should be very easy to know because there is but one person who is to occupy first place in our lives—and that is the Lord Jesus Christ; for did He not mean it when He said, "I am the first"? If He is not put first in our lives, then He does not want to have any place or part in us.

Yet let us see that there is still another meaning to the Lord Jesus being the first. And that is that He is the Originator of all things. In all things and all ways and all plans in our life, do we go to the Lord first and seek to know His mind or seek to let Him originate everything; or do we plan out everything ourselves and leave Him totally out of it? Is Christ Jesus the first, that is to say, the Originator of all things? Individually speaking, this should always be true. Corporately speaking, this ought also to be true in the church. Do we put our heads together in the church and first try to originate and do things, or do we all bow our knees together and pray to know Christ's mind so that He may be the first in the church? Is that not most practical?

Let us now come to the second part of the Son of man's opening declaration of explanation when laying His right hand upon His fallen-down-as-dead disciple John and saying: "Fear not; I am [also] the last." What does this second aspect of His opening words mean? To me it simply means this: that He is the end and purpose of everything. And that by His being the end and the purpose of everything, He obtains all the glory. That glory of His goes forth to you, but then it returns back to Him: that is to say, Christ's glory does not remain in *your* hands but returns to Him, because He is the last and gets the last word.

The risen, ascended Son of man rightfully receives all the glory, since He is the purpose and end of everything. Who, therefore, has the last word in your life? You or Christ?

In our Christian walk on this earth there are many conflicts in which, for example, the flesh strives against the Spirit and the Spirit against the flesh; but who, in the end, has the last word? Sometimes when we Christians get together and we commence arguing or complaining, with everybody wanting to have the last word on a given matter, who ends up getting the last word, you or you or you, or will it be Christ? Whose purpose or will is going to prevail, yours or Christ's? To whom shall go all the glory—you or the Lord?

There is still one final and important dimension, aspect or facet to this first of three elements which are to be found in the explanation given by the risen, ascended Son of man as to the meaning of that tenfold description of the glorified Head of the church which John so fully described when detailing what he saw in his vision on Patmos Isle. And it is reflected in the *total* opening declaration of the Lord here: "I am not only the first, I am also the last." In other words, the glorified Head of the church is, and is to be, everything that is *in between*. Please be advised that it does not mean that He is the first and you are the second. You, of course, consider yourself very humble and are therefore willing to be the second—but not the third. I am not saying this as a joke, for we all very well know that this is a factual description of the attitude too many of us possess.

Whenever we brothers and sisters come together, such an attitude prompts us to say, "Yes, of course, I will let the Lord be the first; for I am ready and willing to obey Him because He most certainly is first. Yes, indeed, He is first, but I am the second." Brethren, there are too many seconds among us believers. Let us be clear here that Jesus' declaration, "I am the first and the last," simply means this: "I am everything. I am the 1st, 2nd, 3rd, 4th, 5th, 6th, and on and on and on to the very last. To put it most concisely—and Biblically—I am all and in all; I am everything in everything; I am everything to every person. In short, I am the All-Inclusive One" (see Ephesians 1:23b; Colossians 3:11b).

Please be advised that this is not a theory. On the contrary, please be reminded again that this all-inclusiveness of the glorified Head of the church is the eternal will of God. Christ's all-inclusiveness is the very content of our testimony as the church. If we wish to manifest a pure testimony concerning Jesus, then that is precisely what it is to be. It does not mean that in our individual lives Christ has a place but only part of a place. Not so; rather, it means that we will let Him be everything in everything—that he must be all and in all.

On the other hand, speaking collectively, this all-inclusive character of Christ means to the church that He as the glorified Head must likewise be everything in everything—He is, and must be, all in all in the church. And if such be the case, then that constitutes a pure church testimony. Anything in the church that is not of Him, anything that is not spelled with the letters of *His* alphabet, anything which comes in without Him—surely all of that will be burned away. The day shall come, in fact, when the First—even the glorified Son of man—shall appear and shall consume everything that is not spelled with His all-inclusive alphabet.

Oh, it bears repeating that the eternal will of God is that Christ may be all and in all to His church as well as to us individually. I wonder, is that true of us? Allow me to say that it was not true of John the beloved disciple who, though quite advanced in spiritual life, and yet, when confronted himself with the all-inclusive testimony concerning Jesus, fell down as one dead.

Is that not surprising, for we will recall that this very apostle had been so close to Jesus his Master during the days of the Lord's humiliation on earth that John had the freedom to lay his head against Jesus' breast. Indeed, John had been that close, intimate and friendly with the Son of man. Nevertheless, when this most senior disciple of His saw Him in His glory as Head of the church, he fell down to the ground as one dead. Can we discern the difference here? If we should truly see the testimony concerning Jesus—if by God's grace we should have revealed to us the Son of man in glory as the glorious Head to us His body, His church—then the very first reaction will be that we must fall down as one dead, even as did Jesus' beloved disciple who by this time had very much advanced in spiritual life. Indeed, can any one of us be compared favorably with the apostle John? I do not believe so; and yet, even this apostle of such great spiritual stature had to fall down as one dead when he beheld the Son of man in glory.

Now why did John react this way? I believe, first of all, that he realized that all his comeliness—whatever he could boast to himself about in terms of what he possessed of goodness and virtue—had immediately turned to corruption upon his seeing such a glorious Christ. All of that could not even begin to be compared with the Lord. It all fell so far short of the glory of Christ that all of it had to go down into death. And secondly, John had to fall down when in the presence of the glorious Lord because whatever belongs to ourselves must go into death. Oh, we can be so alive in ourselves—that is, in our flesh—that we even descend into boasting about such. And the reason is that we have not seen the Lord of glory. If we ever do see Him by revelation, then all things we possess in ourselves will instantly go down into death. They simply must.

Oh, if we truly see what the testimony regarding Jesus is—that He is the All-Inclusive One, the First and the Last—then under *that* light we shall find that all our comeliness has turned to corruption. It will be like what happened with God's beloved servant Daniel: when he saw the glory of the Lord, he acknowledged that all his comeliness had turned to corruption and that there was nothing praiseworthy left in him (Daniel 10:8). The only response is for us to allow ourselves—like John

The Meaning of the Vision

and Daniel—to be raised from the dead by the gracious touch and resurrection power of the Lord.

Now the second element of three in the glorified Son of man's explanation as to the meaning of the tenfold description of himself, which John had so fully described of what he saw in the Patmos vision, was this: "I am the living one." I am reminded here of Saul of Tarsus (later named Paul) who had treated the Lord Jesus as a dead person, as one who had been crucified and who was now very much dead. Saul had therefore logically concluded that a dead man could never pose a threat to him, that he could in fact do anything to that dead man and his reputation and the latter could never respond in return. Even a little baby can strike a dead man and not be struck back in return. But one day this man Saul, on his way to Damascus to take captive this dead man's followers, discovered that the one whom he considered dead and of no worth or value was very much alive. Indeed, Jesus is the Living One. He is the risen Lord in glory. And when Saul met that Man on the Damascus road, he fell down as though dead.

How foolish it is for people to say that God—even God the Son—is dead. He is not dead. He is the Living One. What is the meaning of His being the Living One? It means more than that the Son of man is alive. Yes, Jesus is alive, for did He not declare to Martha: "I am the resurrection and the life"? And did He not also declare: "I am the way, the truth and the life, and no man comes to the Father but by Me"? (see John 11:25a, 14:6a) Yes, indeed, the Son of man is very much alive; even so, to be the Living One means more than just having life. This title also conveys the thought of life in action, life in expression.

By declaring that He is the Living One the Lord is saying the following: "I am life and I am very much alive. I am displaying myself, expressing myself in many ways—and wanting to do so through My disciples individually and wanting to do so also collectively through My body, the church. I am therefore the Living One in action." Do we know the Lord as the Living One?

The great German reformer of Christianity in his day, Martin Luther, was in great trouble and in grave danger for his life. He had been verbally attacked by many of the people, by the Roman Catholic cardinals, and by many others. And there came a day in his life when he felt that all his troubles were too much for him to bear any longer. He could not see any way out. How could just one person like himself continue to stand up against all the opposing world? Luther's faith, in other words, had faltered. He felt himself so weakened and so pressed down by his environment and by all the problems and burdens then weighing upon his shoulders, that he could no longer bear it. He had grown very despondent and was in constant despair and continually sighing over his plight.

Luther's wife, of course, could not avoid observing his condition and wanted very much to cheer him up, but she did not know what to do; nevertheless, God eventually gave his wife wisdom: she put on a black mourning garment as her dress for the day. And so, dressed like that, she came into the presence of Martin Luther; and when he saw her, he inquired as follows: "What happened? Who is dead? Who is dead? What happened?" His wife quietly answered: "God is dead." Luther exclaimed in response: "That cannot be! God cannot die! He is the Living One!" And from this incident he learned a great spiritual lesson; for he began to have his understanding opened, leading him eventually to comment: "Well, now, why should I be worried any longer? Why should I look at myself anymore as though I am able to shoulder the whole world myself and solve all its problems, but forget that the Lord is the Living One? He is living, and if He is living, why should I worry and be discouraged? I can trust in Him and He will perform whatever is necessary."

Oh, let us allow God to reign. How much we need this message! Christ is the Living One; therefore, let us not look at

The Meaning of the Vision

ourselves any longer; for all which we can find there is our weakness. Let us also not look at others; for all which we can find there are faults of various kinds. We are all, in fact, experts in fault-finding, but only finding fault in others and not in ourselves. Let us likewise not look at our environment. That will only disappoint and discourage us. Instead of looking in these flawed directions, let us constantly bear in mind but this one solution to all our problems and difficulties: we have a Lord who is the Living One.

If we will only go to the Lord Jesus we shall find that because He is the Living One, His life is more than sufficient to solve all our problems and to meet all our needs on any and every occasion. Is the Lord the Living One in our life? Let His life in us flow out. Let His life in us express itself. And let us allow Him to be glorified. So when we have problems, difficulties, burdens, or when we are confronted with matters we cannot solve—let us go to the Lord Jesus and say, "Lord, You are the Living One. You are very much alive. In fact, You live in me. I am therefore trusting You and the power of Your life and shall let Your life swallow up everything not of You." And our response as the church should be the same: that we go to the Lord together so that He may lift the church out of all deadness into His living fullness, for He is the Living One.

The third and final element in the glorified Son of man's explanation to John regarding the meaning of the tenfold description of himself in the Patmos vision was as follows: "I became dead, and behold, I am living forever and ever, and I have the keys of death and of hades." The meaning here in this part of the Lord's explanatory declaration to John is this: He is the Victorious One. When it comes right down to the matter, what is life on earth? Life on earth is not a smooth circumstance, for does it not consist of many problems, conflicts, challenges, and struggles? Observe the earthly life of Jesus. His was not an easy life. In fact, He lived a most difficult one—much more difficult than that of anybody else. And yet, He overcame everything which came His way needing to be overcome. He even overcame death, the very last enemy of man and God (II Timothy 1:10b, I Corinthians 15:26).

Here we read that the risen, ascended Son of man first acknowledged to John: "I became dead." Yes, He became dead, but then He immediately added: "I am living forever and ever, and I have the keys of death and of hades." Now if a person has keys he is in control of a given situation. And that is the meaning here in relation to the Lord Jesus, for He has not only the key to the kingdom of heaven but He also now has the controlling keys to death and hades. Even death and hades are under His full control. And thus, He is the All-Victorious One.

Now that is the message the glorified Son of man as Head wished to bring to His body, the church. Do we who are members of His body see the Lord Jesus as the All-Victorious One? If so, we need not fear; let us not fear, because He is the Victorious One—He is the Conqueror. And furthermore, the apostle Paul has declared that in the face of diverse difficulties, troubles, and trials of all kinds—and even in the face of the threat of death itself—we have been made "more than conquerors through Him who loved us" (see Romans 8:37).

Is this, then, our total testimony today? Do we know Christ as the All-Inclusive One? Do we know Him as the Living One? Do we know Him as the Victorious One? As a matter of fact, is that the impression we give to the world that Christ is truly everything to us? Further, is the impression we give to the world that of our testifying to the reality that Christ is the Living One—that there is the expression of His life in us? Or is it the case that there is not much of His life in us? Or do we testify to the reality that Christ is the All-Victorious One?

By way of conclusion, I would like for us to see that so far as the *purpose* of God is concerned Christ is the First and the Last, that so far as the *pattern* of God is concerned He is the Living One, and that so far as the *power* of God is concerned He holds the keys of death and of hades. And that is the meaning

The Meaning of the Vision

of the vision which John on Patmos Isle saw and gave witness to regarding the tenfold description of the glorified Son of man as Head of the church.

May the Lord enable us to hear what the Spirit of God is saying to His church.

Chapter Four

The Seven Golden Lampstands

> The mystery of the seven stars which thou hast seen on [or, in] my right hand, and the seven golden [lampstands].—The seven stars are angels of the seven [churches]; and the seven [lampstands] are seven [churches].
>
> Revelation 1:20

In our previous considerations together thus far on just the first chapter of the book of Revelation, we came to see that the vision which was given to the apostle John on Patmos Isle consisted of the risen, ascended, glorified Son of man standing among seven golden lampstands—they representing seven local churches situated in the Roman province of Asia (Minor)—and which had been identified by their names earlier in the same first chapter. And this remarkable scene was followed immediately by a tenfold description of the glorified Son of man, as delineated and recorded for us by John. It was nothing less than a spiritual presentation of Christ in glory. And then the Spirit of God continued by unveiling for John the condition of these local Asian church assemblies.

Now let us always bear in mind that we who are Christ's followers must see the Lord first and then see the church. For if we see the church first without having seen the Lord, the result can be disastrous, perhaps even tragic. So many of God's people today are looking about trying not only to find the church of God but also wandering here and there in search of the perfect church—that is, the church that will meet their expectations. Or, to phrase it differently, the church that in their opinion will meet God's qualifications. Were they to wander all over the world, they would not be able to find it. The more people wander and search, the more they shall be disappointed. And thus it can be disastrous to their faith. Let us therefore never attempt to see the church first; instead, always see the Lord first; for if you see Him, you will see the church. Seek Him first, and if you find Him, you shall find His church.

There is a continuation of this vision given to John as recorded in chapters 2 and 3, for there we read of the individual condition of each of those seven Asian churches. But before delving into that in our consideration today, I would like for us to concentrate on just verse 20 of the first chapter. We learn from that verse that the glorified Son of man explains to the apostle John the mystery surrounding two things which the apostle saw in the vision of the Lord of glory: He is seen holding in His right hand seven stars and He is observed walking among the seven golden lampstands. Nothing is explained except the identity of those two things: the seven stars and the seven lampstands.

Why is it that the mystery of the seven stars and the seven lampstands is explained to John—and by extension, to all who shall read this book of Revelation? Is it not because these stars and lampstands bear such intimate relationship with the testimony of Jesus? It is as though the Lord were very much concerned that without knowing the identity of these stars and lampstands, the testimony concerning Jesus can neither be understood nor be manifested and realized. These two elements are apparently so important to the testimony of Jesus that without knowing their meaning the testimony of Jesus has no way forth, has no way to be fulfilled. Is it not therefore because of this that the mystery is explained by the Lord here?

Hence, the Lord makes clear to John that the seven golden lampstands are the seven churches or assemblies in the Roman province of Asia (part of modern-day Turkey) and which had already been named by the Lord earlier (1:11). At the time that John saw this vision it was towards the close of the first century and the gospel had already been preached and spread throughout much of that Roman province situated along the Aegean Sea.

Now throughout this province of Asia there were many churches in many different cities, and out of all of them in existence there the Spirit of God selected seven of those local assemblies or churches. And the Spirit of God used these seven as representative of all the local churches through all the ages and throughout the world. In other words, those seven golden lampstands in the vision represented the seven selected churches in Asia, that in turn were meant to represent the entire church of God throughout the universe.

It was mentioned before that the church is both vessel and instrument for holding and disseminating the testimony of Jesus, for the testimony of Jesus is that which matters most to God. His heart is centered exclusively upon the testimony of Jesus because the fulfillment of His eternal purpose is dependent upon the outcome of the testimony of Jesus. And hence, in order that the testimony of Jesus might be maintained and spread forth on this earth God was in need of a vessel and instrument for achieving that objective; and that combined vehicle, may I phrase it that way, is the church. Consequently, God wants us not only to know the testimony concerning His Son but also to experience it, and not only to experience it but to manifest it to the world around us as well.

What, then, is the church? I believe we all know very well that the church is not a physical building. Is this building in which we meet called a church? People do; but if so, it is a great error, because this physical building is not a church. This building may be used by the church and may even be inhabited by the church, but it is not the church. The church is neither a physical building nor an institution nor an organization, but is that which is made up of people. It may be asked, What kind of people? People of every nation, tribe, and language. And in spite of all those differences, they all have one thing in common: they are all redeemed by the precious blood of the Lord Jesus: they all have His life in them. And hence, the church is made up of believers in Christ.

But just a moment, that last assertion is not totally correct. It is quite true that the church is made up of a special kind of people—believers in Christ: redeemed children of God who possess many different backgrounds; but is that the fundamental meaning of what the church is? Do we Christians gathered here, who are marked by so many differences—in culture and background, in education and profession, in ideas and opinions, in temperament and so on—do we constitute what is the definition of the church? If that be the case, then it needs to be asked: With all those differences, how can we be one? For as was made clear earlier, the church *is* one, despite all such differences among all believers who do indeed make up the church. What, then, *is* the church at its most basic, fundamental core? A clue is provided for us by Scripture itself.

The clue as to what is the basic meaning or definition of the church is to be found in the adjective attached to the word lampstand in Exodus 25 and to its plural counterpart, lampstands, here in Revelation 1: the adjective golden. The defining constituent make-up of the church—whether speaking figuratively in terms of the one lampstand or of the seven lampstands—is determined by the symbolic meaning which Scripture gives to that word golden. For these lampstands consist of but one material alone: gold, pure gold, and nothing else. And as has been made clear before, gold in Scripture stands for the nature and glory of God, for the nature of pure gold is that which is precious, incorruptible, and among all metals the most valuable. We may therefore conclude that the church—represented by those *golden* lampstands in the Patmos vision—is made up or consists of actually but one uniting element: Christ the Son of God. And how?—Christ in you, Christ in me, and Christ in each other.

Let us bear in mind, however, that though the defining characteristic of what is truly the church is Christ in each and all of us who are His followers, nevertheless, if we wish to see the authentic church and to see her working and functioning properly, we must all be willing to deny our selves; because the church, as was just made clear, does not consist of *two* materials—Christ and one's self—but of only a single material: Christ himself alone.

The trouble with the church today is not that there is no Christ but that the church today is Christ and I, and probably, with many people, the order is reversed: I and Christ. Is that not the truth? That is why, where there is no cross, there is no appearing of the true church. Unless the cross is allowed to work in each of our lives, the church can never be seen nor truly function as she should. Hence, if she is to be the true church, she not only must be made up of but the one material of Christ and Him alone, but she also must be a beaten work, as was the case with the one golden lampstand of Exodus 25 which God had commanded Moses to make and beat into shape, along with its various cups (shaped like almonds), knobs, and flowers (vv. 31, 33, 36).

Why must the believers who make up the church be beaten? In other words, why must the cross work in believers' lives? Why must the Holy Spirit so order and arrange our circumstances that we must suffer for some reason? It is for the purpose of incorporating Christ more and more into us, for the purpose of purging away our self-life so that Christ himself can be manifested through us. That is the work of the cross; and Exodus 25 further tells us that the one golden lampstand was to have seven branches with "cups shaped like almonds" attached to each branch, along with knobs and flowers—"all [made] of one beaten work of pure gold" (again, see vv. 31, 33, 36). So we see here that the cups mentioned were to be beaten into shape like almond blossoms, and accompanied with knobs and flowers that were likewise made of beaten gold.

Now what thought is God wishing to convey by means of these cups? Does that word not remind us of Psalm 23: "my cup runneth over" (v. 5b)? I believe this word cup in Scripture is meant to convey the idea of portion. The Lord is my cup, is my portion, is my possession, is mine. As the Spirit of God works and works in our lives He will continue to do so until we take upon ourselves the form of a cup. That is to say, until Christ is contained in us, until Christ becomes our portion.

Let us also take note that the shape of these cups are those of almond blossoms with knobs and flowers attached to them. We may be aware that whenever almond is mentioned in the Bible it conveys the thought of resurrection. In the Song of Solomon, for instance, we learn at one point in the narrative that the almond tree has blossomed—the expression of which means that the winter is over and spring has arrived. It also means to convey the thought that darkness and death are over and that therefore resurrection has come to me, since the almond tree was the very first one in Israel which blossomed forth after winter. So we see portrayed here cups that are shaped like almond blossoms accompanied with knobs and flowers.

Now what is a knob? A knob is that which gathers to itself all the riches of the life of the tree of which it is a part, and further, that out of that gathering of the riches of life, flowers blossom forth. And hence, the beauty of the tree is being displayed for all to see.

Is that not a good and pleasant picture of what a church ought to be—of what a church truly is? The church gathers to herself the riches of the life of Christ, and because there is such an abundance of the deposit of divine life, she blossoms forth and produces the fruit of delicious almond nuts. That is to say, the ministry of the church comes forth by the power of Christ's resurrection in her. Is that not what the church is to be like? Is that not how the testimony of Jesus is to go forth? Such is what the authentic church is. And so, in representative fashion, we see in the Patmos vision those seven golden lampstands: each standing in its place, each filled with Christ, and in the power of His resurrection each giving forth the testimony of Jesus in each particular place. It is such a glorious picture that I do not know how to describe it sufficiently; nevertheless, if we can see it in our spirits it will uplift us.

What therefore *is* the church? For the answer let us turn to Ephesians 1: 22-23, where we are told that God has put all things under the feet of the Lord Jesus and given Him to be Head over all things to the assembly (that is, to the church) which is His body, the fullness of Him who fills all in all. *That in the most concise terms is what the church truly is.* God has made Christ the Head over all things in heaven and earth and under the earth—everything. He has made Christ head over all things to His church which is His body—the fullness of Him who fills all in all. Now, therefore, Christ is the Head, but where is the body? His body is the church.

When you meet a person, which part of him do you see first? When you look at that person, do you see his feet first, see His body first, or see His face—His head—first? If you see a person by looking at some part of his body first, you will never know him; but should you first see his face or head, immediately you know him. Or should you look at a part of that person's body first and try to guess what that person looks like, you will find him to be very much unlike your guess. That person does not look like that at all. You may try to do that, but you end up grossly mistaken. If, however, you see the person's head first, everything will be crystal clear as to what that person looks like or is known to be. Consequently, that is why we must see the head first. If we see the Head, then we know that Person; otherwise, we shall never recognize Him as the Universal Man.

What is the meaning of Christ as the Head over everything? The meaning of Him as Head is that He is full of riches. Oh, the inexhaustible riches of the Head! He is the source of all supply for He is the fountain and therefore He is the Head over everything. But what, then, is the body? The body—the church—*contains* the riches of the Head and the body *expresses* the greatness of the Head. The Lord Jesus is the Head, therefore, and all the fullness of the Godhead—all the unsearchable riches of Christ—dwell in Him bodily.

And hence, Christ the Head is seeking for a body to complement himself: to contain, express, and manifest himself. And Christ the Head finds that in the church as His body. Both the Head and the body are one, because both Head and body share the same life, and thus both are constituted as one. Indeed, the combined Head and body are one person or personality. That, then, is what is meant by the church when combined with the Head. The church and Christ as Head are one. They are united by the one divine life they share, by the one divine nature they share together (II Peter 1:4b).

They are constitutionally one: one in fellowship and one in personality. We as His body the church are not here to present a personality of our own while the Lord as Head separately maintains His personality. Not so; instead, the church is to express the personality of the Head—Christ—because they are one; which signifies that what the Head is, is what the body is.

As was pointed out before, if there is any discrepancy, contradiction, difference between Head and body—if the body has something foreign in it which the Head does not know or recognize as being of His nature—then the testimony of Jesus will be adversely affected. But if the body is filled with the riches of the Head, then the body will give forth the strongest possible testimony of Jesus as Head.

Someone may ask, Why do we find being mentioned here in Revelation *seven* golden lampstands? Why not have just one mentioned? For the Head is one, so His body is one. According to nature, there cannot be one head and two or more bodies. So, with Christ and the church, there must be but one Head and His one body.

By way of further explanation for why there are seven lampstands mentioned and not simply one, we must review

The Seven Golden Lampstands

some Old Testament-era history. We may recall that in the tabernacle of old there was only one golden candlestick or lampstand in the holy place, but it had seven branches: one lampstand with seven branches: all seven branches, yet they were all one—seven but one (see Exodus 25). So if there is to be consistency between both Testaments, why, then, does this Patmos vision not have simply one golden lampstand, as was the case in the Old Testament period, instead of there being seven golden lampstands? Actually there is no difference or inconsistency here in the New Testament book of Revelation. It is simply a difference in emphasis. Whereas in the Old Testament times there were these seven branches all united into one lampstand by the base, here in this New Testament prophetic vision the seven individual lampstands are all united by the glorified Son of man who is walking among and around them, thus uniting them all into one. Let us also bear in mind that the number seven in the Scriptures represents completeness and perfection. Accordingly, although there are seven golden lampstands present, they are nonetheless all united into one testimony by Christ the glorified Son of man.

Then what is the difference in emphasis? Simply stated, whereas in the Old Testament the emphasis was on *unity*—the unity of God's people, here in the New, it is on the matter of *responsibility* in spreading the testimony of Jesus locally. It by no means signifies that these seven golden lampstands are not united. They are indeed united—by Christ—for the church is one. They are not united by government, by organization, by leadership, or whatever else it may be. They are not united by such means. Yes, they are physically independent, separate, local assemblies, with each standing on its own responsibility for spreading the testimony of Jesus in each's own geographical area, but it does not mean that their unity is disrupted and that they are *spiritually* independent of each other. On the contrary, they are related together in Christ, in that there is a spiritual unity which unites them all in Christ. The unity is still there but it is being expressed by the Son of man because He is shown in the Patmos vision standing and walking in the midst of the seven lampstands. In other words, the Lord unites all seven into himself. So, actually it is the same vision in both Testaments, the only difference being one of emphasis.

Nevertheless, when speaking of the matter of responsibility, we must observe that each local church or assembly must bear its own responsibility. Thus, though all saints in all local churches throughout the world are one in Christ Jesus, the testimony of Jesus on earth today has been given to all the local churches wherever God's people assemble in the name of the Lord Jesus. Hence, that explains why in the Patmos vision there are seven lampstands, each standing on its own. Which is to say, therefore, that each local church is responsible for spreading and fulfilling the testimony of Jesus in each locality where situated, though in spirit all the saints in all these local churches have been joined into one by the one Lord and Savior of all.

If, for instance, the Lord has put you saints here in New York and even though you are spiritually united with all the saints in all the churches of God in different places around the world, nevertheless, God holds you responsible for maintaining and spreading the testimony of Jesus here in New York. You cannot, for example, depend upon the assembly in Washington for the fulfilling of the testimony of Jesus here. God holds each assembly of His people responsible. That, therefore, is why here in Revelation chapter 1, instead of there being presented one lampstand with seven branches as in the Old Testament tabernacle and temple, there are seven lampstands presented but all united by the Son of man walking in their midst, and yet each assembly lampstand being held accountable for its responsibility in fulfilling the testimony of the Lord in each one's area.

We must never forget that the church of God is one. The church is universal in scope, by which is meant that the church

The Seven Golden Lampstands

includes all who are believers, who have been redeemed by the grace of God through the blood of Christ Jesus. The church is one spiritually; even so, the testimony of the oneness of the body—the testimony of Jesus—is maintained on this earth today by local assemblies situated in many places throughout the world. Let us therefore not be so spiritual that we so spiritualize the church as being heavenly that she has simply vanished from the earth into heaven, we thus claiming that the church is invisible, intangible, untouchable, and therefore she is in heaven and no longer on earth. For we are still in the flesh, not yet having arrived at that end-time moment of taking upon the promised spiritual body whereby space and time are no longer problems due to our having entered Eternity. Yes, indeed, we all look forward to that day; but in the here and now on earth, time and space present great burdens to us, because if we are here we cannot be there; and hence, we are bound and limited by space and time within the locality where God has placed us in the local church for bearing the responsibility of fulfilling the testimony of His Son Jesus. On the other hand, let us not be so earthly-minded with regard to the church that we end up lacking that essential heavenly vision.

Yes, we must acknowledge that on the one hand, there is the principle of the church being heavenly in nature; for it is quite true that her calling or vocation is heavenly. The church *is* spiritual and she *is* universal in scope in terms of her redeemed ones throughout the ages. On the other hand, today the church is an earthly instrument carrying out a heavenly testimony. She can be seen, she can be touched, she can experience fellowship. The church, in this regard, may be strange to us, but I firmly believe that this is the Lord's purpose in the church on earth.

Consequently, at the beginning of the book of Revelation we see those seven selected local churches in the Roman province of Asia; we do *not* see the one church universal as could have been represented by one golden lampstand. Instead of that we see seven lampstands representative of those seven chosen churches in Asia Minor. Whereas the glorified Son of man is presented in these early chapters of Revelation as dealing with those seven local churches or assemblies, He is *not* seen dealing with the universal church; however, we will notice when coming to the book's *final two chapters* that we no longer see the church in Ephesus, we no longer see the church in Smyrna, we no longer see the church in Pergamum, nor the church in Thyatira, nor the church in Sardis, nor the church in Philadelphia, nor the church in Laodicea. Nor, it can be said, would we see the church in New York or the church in Hong Kong or the church in Sydney, etc., etc. We do not see all these local churches in those final chapters; rather, what we there behold is the one church universal: there she shines in glory, for she is the one golden lampstand shining in her brightness and uplifting the testimony of Jesus forever and ever throughout Eternity.

Let us therefore never lose sight of the vision of the one church universal manifesting the glory of God in Eternity, for this is what God is ultimately after: this has been His glorious purpose from before the foundation of the world—indeed, from eternity past. Hence, there in those final chapters of Revelation, we take note that the body of Christ is completed, that the body is fully united to the Head—the bride to the bridegroom. And there we also see that the church shines in the glory of the Head. Let me say again that we must never lose sight of *that* vision, because if we do, we shall be finished and done for spiritually: being full of disappointment and despair. But by maintaining *that* vision, hope of God's eventual fulfillment springs eternal.

On the other hand, we need to ask ourselves this: How is that ultimate vision to be realized? How does God work to bring all that about? Simply put, He works through the local assemblies. God through the glorified Son of man is dealing with every assembly in every place. As a matter of fact, that is what is being presented to John and to us by means of the earlier vision in Revelation: the glorified Lord walking among those seven lampstands. Now *that* is where and how the building up of the church is taking place. The Lord is not building some imaginary, invisible castle in the air. He is instead building right here on earth with you and me and with every local church around the world. This vision is therefore most practical in its implications. The Lord is working to build the church here on earth, and through such building there will finally be realized and completed that which God's heart has been set upon from eternity past.

In view of all this, we may say that the church universal is the church local and that the church local is the church universal. These are merely two aspects of the building up of the one body of Christ. One is principle, the other is practice; and when these two are put together, the body is realized and completed. And that explains why, at the beginning of the book of Revelation, instead of there being shown the church universal with but *one* lampstand being presented—which would be reflective of God's principle, there is instead presented to John (and to us) *seven* lampstands representative of those seven assemblies in Asia Minor, which are reflective of God's practice. Whereas the final vision in Revelation is heavenly in principle, this prophetic book's earliest vision is earthly and very practical. And hence, the testimony of Jesus is very much bound up with, and related to, the seven golden lampstands which—explained the risen, ascended, glorified Son of man—are the seven local churches in Asia Minor.

There is no time left today to discuss together the implications for us of the Son of man's explanation to John as to what the mystery surrounding the seven stars in His right hand signified. That will have to await our next time together.

Chapter Five

The Seven Stars

> The mystery of the seven stars which thou hast seen on [or, in] my right hand, and the seven golden [lampstands].—The seven stars are angels of the seven [churches]; and the seven [lampstands] are seven [churches].
>
> Revelation 1:20
>
> The spirit of prophecy is the testimony of Jesus.
>
> Revelation 19:10e

Today I would like for us to consider together the second mystery which the glorified Son of man explained to His bondman John—that of the seven stars which He held in His right hand. What is the explanation of these stars? What do they represent?

In reading the writings of various Bible commentators and expositors you will most likely end up lost in the forest. One of them will inform you that the stars represent this and another will write, No, the stars represent that, and so on; in fact, all of them are quite certain what the mystery concerning these stars is. Upon learning what they all have to say, however, those stars end up remaining a mystery to you!

But let us not be dismayed any longer, for the Lord has himself explained the matter already: these seven stars, He announced to John, are the messengers or angels of the seven churches. The Greek New Testament word for angel can just as legitimately be translated into English as messengers. And hence, the angels serve as messengers for God, and thus, these messengers can be called, and *are* called, angels.

So regardless what may be the various interpretations of all these commentators and expositors, I believe one thing becomes quite clear: that these stars represent those who are spiritually responsible for the testimony of Jesus in their various churches.

Accordingly, we may say that these seven stars are the messengers of the seven churches—they represent the spiritually responsible element in the church; and this I will explain a little bit later today. What I wish us to consider right now is this: Why is it that the Lord Jesus, in sending these seven letters to the seven churches, did not write to those churches *directly* but instead addressed them all and delivered them all into the hands of these seven angels?

In contrast to that, we will notice that the Lord, through the apostle Paul, had written letters previously and much earlier which were addressed to the churches at Rome, Corinth, in Galatia, at Ephesus, Philippi, Colosse, and Thessalonica. But in His commissioning through Paul that those letters be written and sent out, we find that in the salutations of them all they were addressed to the churches directly—that is to say, they were addressed directly, for example, to the saints who were in Rome or to those who were believers and faithful ones in the Lord in Corinth, etc., etc. Those letters were each and all addressed to each and all of those churches as a whole and to each and all of those churches directly. Furthermore, in the Philippian letter, when responsible elders and deacons are being mentioned, it is done so in connection *with* the saints, not *without* the saints. So we find that in His first letters which the Lord wrote to His churches—and in this case through His apostle Paul—each of them was addressed directly and to the particular local church as a whole.

But we shall notice that there is something different about the second set of letters which the Lord Jesus sent to His church—in this case, through the apostle John: for He did not address them directly but indirectly to the messenger of each local church and, through the messenger, to each of those churches. Now why? An understanding of this is very important. At the time when the Lord Jesus sent His letters to those various churches by the hand of Paul, it could be said that they were in their normal condition. In other words, they were in a more or less normal state in spite of the fact that they were marked by problems and/or difficulties. For instance, in Corinth many problems existed—yet in one sense the saints there were still in a relatively normal condition as a local church, with the Lord dealing and disciplining the church as necessary. Indeed, He was trying to preserve the believers in the Corinthian church from becoming *ab*normal; nevertheless, it could be said that in general the church was still normal, with the Lord dealing directly with the churches during that period.

Let us recognize, however, that at the time of the apostle John it was towards the end of the Apostolic Age, with the church in general having declined to the point that the various churches had most all of them become abnormal. Now to us in our day their abnormality would probably still appear to be normal, were we to compare ourselves with them. However, in the eyes of the Lord the church at that time had already sunk to a most serious abnormal state; so serious in fact, that the Lord would no longer deal directly with the churches but would only deal with those who were in a spiritual position of responsibility, and thus through them would He now have dealings with the churches.

Here I would pose a series of questions for all of us to ponder over quite seriously. Is it in the thought of God that all the members of the local expression of the body of Christ ought to be responsible to the Head in regard to the testimony of His Son Jesus? Can we ever say as truth that there is any brother or any sister in a local church who had *no* responsibility in relation to the testimony of Jesus in that church? Can anyone who is saved sit back and inwardly, if not outwardly, say: "Well, now, you others just go ahead and bear the responsibility concerning the testimony of Jesus, and I will simply withdraw and watch and enjoy from the sidelines." Can any of us actually think this? Is that the thought of the Head of the body? Can that at all be the genuine thinking of the body? Can any of us imagine that such an idea is a true representation of the thought of the body of Christ? Certainly not! We know full well that in the original thought of God every member of the body of Christ locally is to be a living, functioning member thereof, that each one is responsible for the spread of the testimony regarding Jesus in the particular place where he or she may be. In God's thought no one is excepted. No one!

The very nature of life is that of being responsible. If you do not wish to bear any responsibility, do not seek to have spiritual life. For if you are dead, there is no more responsibility. But whenever life comes into being, responsibility automatically comes into being as well. No matter the measure of life anyone has—whether little or much—life's characteristic is that of responsibility: a little life will mean a small amount of responsibility, whereas much more life calls forth greater responsibility. But regardless the measure of life in a person, that life has about it the characteristic of responsibility. It is a principle which no one can deny or avoid. All who are born of God and have the life of the Lord Jesus in them are responsible. The Lord holds all of us responsible for His testimony. Are we not to be concerned with His interests? Are we not to be concerned with souls who are yet unsaved? Are we not to be concerned with the spiritual welfare of God's children? Are we not to be concerned with the business of the Father's house?

None of us can be a Christian and a believing member of the body of Christ without bearing some responsibility. I am not speaking here with regard to responsibility in doing this practical task or doing that one. Rather, I am right now speaking of the spiritual principle that lies behind the practice. Everyone who is brought into the family of God and is a member of the body of Christ in local expression is responsible for the testimony of Jesus in that locale or area. If the testimony of Jesus falls, it is because of you and you and me. And if the testimony stands, it is because of you and you and me. Everyone must share in being spiritually responsible.

What is meant by spiritual responsibility? It is not some work or some duty or some function which people in the church may try to put upon you. How sad to observe that if people in a local assembly do not grant a church member some title or place some work or some service upon this or that member, then that one simply does not perform any service whatsoever. Whatever service or work or function which is carried out is all conducted on the human level; all such man-induced arrangement cannot be deemed to be *spiritual* responsibility. To the contrary, spiritual responsibility in the church is not some labor, service or function placed upon members of the local church by others but is that which is placed upon His saints in the church by the Lord himself. And hence, spiritual responsibility is the expression of life and is the sharing of the burden of the Lord; and in thus sharing the Lord's burden, God's people share in His wisdom and power.

Why is there so little power in the church? It is because Christians are not sharing in the Lord's burden. Spiritual responsibility is a fellowshiping with the Lord in His testimony. Are we not all responsible for that? Can any of us say or think that he or she is but a little member in the body and it therefore does not matter? Can any of us live our life and do so in our own way and believe such conduct will not affect the testimony of Jesus? That we can simply sit back and hope that the testimony of Jesus will go forth and accomplish God's purpose? That is an impossible situation! I do not know how to impress upon us the importance of this; but may the Spirit of the Lord impress this matter deeply upon our hearts. The going forth of the testimony of Jesus is our responsibility.

The Key to "Revelation"

Let us not think that spiritual responsibility rests entirely upon just a few. No, that is not the mind of the Lord. The carrying out of the testimony of Jesus rests upon the whole body of Christ in local expression. That is why those first letters of the Lord sent forth through Paul to the churches were all addressed to each and every one of those churches as a whole; meaning, that everyone in each local church was addressed directly.

How, though, did it come about that as time went by there gradually developed among this second set of churches cited here in the Patmos vision a decline spiritually and that as these churches so declined, this matter of spiritual responsibility gradually became that of only a relatively few saints in nearly all of these churches? How, indeed, did this come about? It apparently was the case that the rest of the believers in these local churches chose merely to come on the Lord's day and sit through and wait till the end of the meeting! This state of affairs is abnormal, very abnormal. Here we observe that the Lord was dealing with the true condition—however abnormal it may have been—by writing to the messengers.

We come now to the matter of the messengers. Who were these messengers? Personally, I believe the term messenger in relation to each of these seven churches is being employed in a collective sense and not individually. Therefore, the mention of each church's messenger (see Revelation 2 and 3) does not mean that there is one person in each local church who is responsible for everything. That would be too regrettable if that should be the case here; nevertheless, I am of the opinion that at this time in the history of these local churches, the declining situation has not reached to that degraded depth yet. So I believe the mention of each church's messenger here is being used in a collective sense. In other words, in each of these seven churches there has gradually developed that the spiritual responsibility of each church had begun to shift and to be concentrated and gathered up into the hands of a few, and that by this time these few seemed to have been shouldering that burden alone before the Lord themselves.

Please notice that there is no mention here of elders or deacons—an indication that the Lord is not dealing here with church office holders or those occupying a formal titled position. The Lord is instead dealing with the reality of the church situation. The Lord is therefore observed here employing the term messenger in a collective sense for each church, and is refraining as well from referring to elders and deacons, because sometimes they may in fact hold those positions of responsibility but spiritually they are not being responsible at all.

The Lord is here addressing himself to the messengers without mentioning any title, position or office. And why? Because He has been compelled by the declining spiritual condition of these churches to deal with the actual situation. In any local church there must be some who are the ones bearing spiritual responsibility in relation to the testimony of Jesus for that church. They have not been appointed by man nor may they even be recognized by man. And though they may not occupy any official position in the local church, nonetheless, they are the ones who are being spiritually responsible.

And those, I believe, are the messengers—indeed, the stars in the right hand of the Son of man. This is not an original thought on my part; nevertheless, to me it is the best understanding of what the Lord of glory had himself explained to John concerning the mystery of those seven stars. And when one connects this thought—of the messengers being those few saints in each church who were the ones actually bearing spiritual responsibility at that time—with the call of overcomers in each of those same seven Asian local churches (see Revelation 2 and 3), then the aforementioned thought becomes clear and makes very good sense. For the call of overcomers is the call to spiritual responsibility, a call to be responsible for the testimony of Jesus in the locale of each local church. Hence, in the Patmos vision the Son of man as Head of the body of Christ was looking for some in each church to respond to the call to overcome, and those who would respond would become part of the make-up of that church's messenger: those who collectively bear spiritual responsibility in relation to fulfilling the testimony of Jesus in each of those seven places.

Let us recall again that in the vision which John saw, the glorified Son of man singled out only two objects from among many features in the vision for explaining their mystery: the seven stars and the seven lampstands. Now those messengers were referred to symbolically by the Lord Jesus as stars. Actual stars are of course celestial, that is, heavenly, bodies; whereas lampstands are earthly instruments. Stars are in heaven, lampstands are on earth; yet both give light. They both are seen giving light in the night, but one shines from above and the other shines from beneath. Now what is the connection between these stars and those seven lampstands? What is the relationship between, on the one hand, those who are spiritually responsible and, on the other hand, the local church as a whole?

In answering this question let us first consult the Old Testament book of Zechariah, chapter 4, where we are given to see another lampstand. The prophet Zechariah was awakened by the Lord and was shown a vision: a golden lampstand appeared with seven pipes, and on the right and on the left of that lampstand the prophet beheld two olive trees and saw these two olive trees pour out their gold through pipes into the bowl of the lampstand; and the word of the Lord Jehovah came forth audibly: "Not by might nor by power, but by my Spirit."

The prophet Zechariah does not understand the meaning of all this. He especially asked twice concerning those two olive trees. Now what or who are they? And why are they there? Moreover, what is their relationship with the golden lampstand? We are told that the two olive trees are "the sons of oil," and they pour forth oil as gold and gold as oil, and that, we may say—in New Testament terminology—is the Spirit of life in Christ Jesus (cf. Romans 8:2a).

Do we now see the connection between star and lampstand? Those who are spiritually responsible in fulfilling the testimony of Jesus in relation to the local church as a whole are those who maintain a heavenly position in Christ. Why is it that some brothers and sisters cannot bear spiritual responsibility even if they wished to do so? It is because they have lost their heavenly position. They are earthbound—incapacitated, as it were, by earthly matters and interests. Indeed, many brothers and sisters seek for those earthly things, their hearts having been enticed by those things; and thus, they are bound by the earth. Having lost their heavenly position in Christ, they are no longer able to bear spiritual responsibility. Yes, they may still be able to do the task appointed by the church so-called for certain service, but they are not in a position to bear *spiritual* responsibility. Consequently, the reality is gone, so far as they are concerned: such brethren can no longer pour forth oil as gold and gold as oil.

Please understand that if you wish to bear spiritual responsibility for the testimony of Jesus, you must be a star. Figuratively speaking, you must remain in heaven; that is to say, you must maintain your position in the heavenlies in Christ Jesus (cf. Ephesians 2:6); and as you maintain that position, the oil of the Spirit comes forth. The oil is gold and the gold is oil. In other words, the life of God is poured forth, and thus, the testimony of the lampstand—the local church—is maintained through the life of Jesus that is poured forth into the church by those who are spiritual lamps.

Bearing spiritual responsibility is not standing here in the assembly and preaching a sermon; it is not going to the basement of the church building and sweeping the floor. These and other such labors are only outward expressions; but the reality is, that those who are spiritually responsible and burdened for God's interests pour forth their life into the church—yet not *their* life but the indwelling life of Christ. And as they pour forth the life of Christ into the lampstand—the local church—we shall find that she is burning and giving forth light.

Here we come to understand that the supply for true church service is heavenly but of course the service is carried out on earth. The stars are above but the lampstands are on earth. Such is the relationship between star and lampstand—between messenger and local church. Oh, that God may raise up many brothers and sisters in many places who are not only willing but eager to pour their gold, their oil—even the indwelling life of Christ—into the various lampstands wherever situated and keep them burning and thus manifesting the testimony of Jesus.

Chapter Six

The Seven Churches

What follows below are the introductory words contained in all seven letters sent by the glorified Son of man to those seven churches selected by the Holy Spirit from among all of the then-existing churches situated in the Roman province of Asia. The complete text of all seven letters appears in Revelation chapters 2 and 3.

To the angel of the [church] in Ephesus write: These things says he that holds the seven stars in his right hand, who walks in the midst of the seven golden [lampstands] (2:1).

And to the angel of the [church] in Smyrna write: These things says the first and last who became dead and lives (2:8).

And to the angel of the [church] in Pergamos write: These things says he that has the sharp two-edged sword (2:12).

And to the angel of the [church] in Thyatira write: These things says the Son of God, he that has his eyes as a flame of fire, and his feet are like fine brass (2:18).

And unto the angel of the [church] in Sardis write: These things saith he that has the seven Spirits of God and the seven stars (3:1a, b).

And to the angel of the [church] in Philadelphia write: These things saith the holy, the true; he that has the key of David, he who opens and no one shall shut, and shuts and no one shall open (3:7).

And to the angel of the [church] in Laodicea write: These things says the Amen, the faithful and true witness, the beginning of the creation of God (3:14).

In addition, what follows below are the repeated calls for overcomers in these same seven letters and their corresponding rewards.

> He that has an ear, let him hear what the Spirit says to the [churches]. To him that overcomes, I will give to him to eat of the tree of life which is in the paradise of God (2:7).
>
> He that has an ear, let him hear what the Spirit says to the [churches]. He that overcomes shall in no wise be injured of the second death (2:11).
>
> He that has an ear, let him hear what the Spirit says to the [churches]. To him that overcomes, to him will I give of the hidden manna; and I will give to him a white stone, and on the stone a new name written, which no one knows but he that receives it (2:17).
>
> And he that overcomes, and he that keeps unto the end my works, to him will I give authority over the nations, and he shall shepherd them with an iron rod; as vessels of pottery are they broken in pieces, as I also have received from my Father; and I will give to him the morning star. He that has an ear, let him hear what the Spirit says to the [churches] (2:26-29).
>
> He that overcomes, he shall be clothed in white garments, and I will not blot his name out of the book of life, and will confess his name before my Father

and before his angels. He that has an ear, let him hear what the spirit says to the [churches] (3:5-6).

He that overcomes, him will I make a pillar in the temple of my God, and he shall go no more at all out; and I will write upon him the name of my God, and the name of the city of my God, the new Jerusalem, which comes down out of heaven, from my God, and my new name. He that has an ear, let him hear what the Spirit says to the [churches] (3:12).

He that overcomes, to him will I give to sit with me in my throne; as I also have overcome, and have sat down with my Father in his throne. He that has an ear, let him hear what the Spirit says to the [churches] (3:21).

As has been referenced repeatedly in our several discussions together thus far on the book of Revelation, we have come to see that the key verse to the entire book is the last part of verse 10 of chapter 19: "the spirit of prophecy is the testimony of Jesus." And during the past few weeks we have come to see from chapter 1 of Revelation the testimony of Jesus—who He is and what He is to us as His church. And in our last time of fellowship together on Revelation we came to understand that God's vessels for the manifestation to the world of that testimony are the Lord's churches situated in various localities throughout the world. And in our discussion today we want to consider together the practical application of this vision which the apostle John saw—that is to say, of what has been revealed concerning the testimony of Jesus in relation to the church. What, in fact, does the Head of the body of Christ find in these seven local churches in relation to the testimony of Jesus? What is the true condition of all these churches in relation to the testimony?

The Key to "Revelation"

With perhaps the exception of the last of these seven churches—that of Laodicea—the Lord found some good things in the other six which He could commend. Every one of those six churches had something good. Some had good works and some had good teachings. As a matter of fact, the Lord notices everything about each local church, for He does not miss anything.

At times you may think the Lord does not notice something good in you and you end up feeling quite sorry about it. It may not matter to you if people do not notice, but if the Lord does not notice, you will feel very bad. Do you have such a feeling sometimes? Please understand that though *man* may miss something, the Lord notices everything. Indeed, in the vision of Revelation He is seen walking in the midst of those seven lampstands, and as He is walking along, his eyes as flames of fire are penetrating into the very hearts of all the saints in those churches and He takes note of everything about them. Nothing is hidden from Him, good or bad. And certainly it is the heart desire of the Lord to notice the good more than the bad.

We, however, are just the opposite. It is very easy for us to notice what is bad in others. It does not require much observation on our part; it seems as if we are born that way. Whereas we can readily notice what is bad in others instantaneously, it seems to be quite difficult for us to notice what is good in others. That takes time. We have to be with someone for more or less a year before we will discover that he is not that bad after all.

The Lord Jesus, on the other hand, delights in noticing what is good. He is not trying to pick out faults. To the contrary, He is not that kind of person. I am reminded of what occurred one day when an elderly lady was going to be baptized and the pastor was questioning her as to her faith. One question which was asked was this: "What is our Lord Jesus doing today in heaven?" And the elderly lady answered, "He is in heaven with eyes wide open, looking at me, and trying to find fault with me."

What a grievous misunderstanding! The Lord is not like that. Yes, He notices everything, including the bad; but He delights in seeing the good. And whenever He sees anything good He commends us for it. And with regard to these churches in Revelation 2 and 3 He mentions good things (except Laodicea) and praises every church for those good things. The Lord is more than willing to commend, to praise, to say something good about every one of those six churches.

Nevertheless, though the Lord notices everything, especially the good things, His heart is not at all in those good things. In every local expression of the church universal there are many good things—some more, some less—and the Lord notices those things, but His heart is not in them. Such was not what He was looking for in those seven churches. What He was actually looking for in each of those local assemblies was simply one item of interest: His testimony. In fact, that one item is a matter of life and death to every local church. If the testimony of Jesus is there, then there is valid reason for the continuation of that church; but if the testimony of Jesus is *not* there, then there is no reason why that local church should be continued, and its lampstand shall be removed in spite of the good things which may be there.

This is a very serious matter. If there is something good in a given local church, we think it justifies that church's continued existence. For the Lord, however, it is entirely different. He is not looking for anything merely good. Yes, such things He can praise, but He cannot be satisfied with those things. The Lord is only looking for one thing in the church which can satisfy Him: and if that thing is in the church, then there is a valid reason for her continued existence; but if the Lord cannot find that, then there is no reason for that church to continue.

It has been mentioned before that if we know what is the basic, fundamental constitution of the church, we readily realize that she is nothing less than the extension and enlargement of

Christ the Head. The church is not something foreign to Him; rather, the church is not anything other than Christ himself; so it is but natural for Christ to look for and find himself in the church. If He cannot find himself there, then that church has forfeited her meaning for continuing to exist. So when we consider the practical application of this vision of the glorified Son of man, we see Him walking among the seven lampstands and looking—we can now conclude—for just one thing: He is looking for himself in these churches.

What a travesty it will be if we should have many activities and labors, and end up working ourselves to death; what a travesty it will be if we should adhere diligently to many teachings that are in fact scriptural and good and perhaps have about them the commendable characteristic of tradition? What a travesty it will indeed be if we should have all these good things—and yet, the Lord cannot find himself in us when He comes into our midst! Oh, how readily we can talk, and talk much, about Him and can do many different things in His name, and yet such work is not of himself: none of that is the expression of His life nor was it done in the energy of His Spirit. In fact, the result of it all is that the world has seen *us* but has not seen the Lord.

Now what if such a circumstance should happen? I myself would feel that such a situation would be most serious and even frightening. In this Patmos vision of John's the Lord was observed walking in the midst of the seven lampstands back then that represented those seven selected local churches in Asia Minor. Let us not therefore think the Lord is no longer walking among the churches today nor that He is not coming into our midst as a church today. Most certainly the Lord continues to do that in our day. It is most assuredly a fact that the Lord is here looking at us.

Now what does He see in us as a local expression of the universal church? Does He find himself in us? Does He find that which answers and corresponds to himself? Does He find that which satisfies himself or will He merely find a great amount of labor, teachings, activities, people, and even well-functioning organization—and all without Him being there? Most likely there will be very little, perhaps even nothing of all of that, which speaks of himself. Consequently, I would inquire of ourselves: What is the actual state of affairs with regard to the testimony of Jesus in our local church today? Is the Lord of glory being seen and manifested in our midst today or is it ourselves that is on display?

This is why the risen, ascended, glorified Son of man begins each of these seven letters sent to those seven local churches with a revelation of himself that describes to each church who He is and what He is. And then He looks to see if there is a reflection of himself in each church based on what He had just then revealed and emphasized to her. That is essentially what He is looking for. The church is to be measured by one thing and one thing only as to whether she is accepted or is rejected—as to whether her lampstand remains or is removed: she is to be measured by the revelation of Christ alone. In other words, each local church is to be measured by whether the testimony of Jesus is present or absent there.

In Revelation 21 we are shown the holy city, the new Jerusalem. We are also shown an angel who has in his hand a golden rod with which he measures everything in that city: the city itself, its wall, and its gates. That measurement is a full and perfect one because the city is foursquare, meaning that the length, height, width, and breadth are all the same. And thus the city measures up fully in exact correspondence with the golden rod which represents Christ himself. In the future the church shall measure up fully and perfectly to the "measure of the stature of the fullness of Christ" (Ephesians 4:13c), and that is what we see in new Jerusalem. But let us realize that prior to new Jerusalem God does not have another and different measurement, because God is measuring us today with the same measurement; and that is the measure of Christ himself.

The Key to "Revelation"

How does the church stand before God? It is determined by only one thing: how much the measure of Christ is in the church; or, to phrase the matter another way, how much of the testimony of Jesus is in correspondence with the revelation of Jesus. That, then, is the one thing which the Lord is looking for. It is a most solemn and serious matter.

There is another matter to be noticed here: the seven churches are very, very different the one from the other. The vision which the apostle John saw was that of seven separate golden lampstands representing seven local expressions of the church universal. And as we have already noted previously, the church is one because the body is one, there being but one head and one body, and not two or more bodies but only one body with one head. Christ is the Head, the church is the body, and the latter includes all who are the Lord's throughout the world and throughout the ages. But so far as the propagation of the testimony of Jesus is concerned, it must be localized, for we human beings are still living in the flesh: if we are in New York City we cannot be in San Francisco.

So in considering our practical responsibility as members of the body of Christ locally, we must realize that those who gather together in one particular place are responsible for the spreading of the testimony of Jesus in that local area. The saints there are a small token of the church universal. That explains why in John's vision there were seven separate golden lampstands. Each was required to stand on its own; that is to say, each local church was responsible for the propagation of the testimony of Jesus in that church's locality—in Ephesus, in Smyrna, and so forth.

With regard to the matter of government and responsibility, each local assembly back then was independent of all the others in existence. Moreover, each local church had its special feature: no two churches were exactly alike. In reading the seven letters sent to those seven churches in Asia Minor, we easily discover that each church was different from all the others. Each had its special characteristics. They all had the same Lord but the expressions of the one Lord were many and various.

This matter is very important for us to understand. Why were these seven churches shown to be quite different from each other in their features? They were shown this way so that the readers of this book of Revelation would come to realize that the feature differences among these were the result of the development of life. If there is life present, there cannot be uniformity. When life is present, its growth and development result in the emergence of different features. That is the nature of life. If what is present is not life but organization it can only result in there being exactly the same features showing up. The resultant features can thus be easily duplicated and multiplied in appearance, with all features emerging exactly the same as at the first.

The local churches cannot be uniform. If we try to make them uniform, we simply turn them into organizations. Life is not present anymore. We must allow them to develop according to the environment within which God has placed them and according to the revelation which God has given them to foster their sets of special features.

We therefore observe these seven churches with seven different sets of features. Their characteristics are not exactly the same. I mention this because we human beings have the tendency to make everything uniform. Is this not the tendency of human nature? Are there not forces in the world which are attempting to make everything uniform? If you and I do not conform then we are not allowed to exist. That is human nature in general. Let us observe our own tendencies. When we find anybody different from us, do we not have the urge and desire to try to change them and conform them to ourselves? Such is human nature.

But with respect to these seven churches, in principle they are the same, in life they are the same, they all have the same

The Key to "Revelation"

Lord as their Head; and yet, how different from one another they are in terms of those special features which they uniquely possess. And such is life: variety, not uniformity. That should be the principle which governs the affairs of each and every local church. A church is not to imitate or copy other local churches. Nor should a local church put other churches under her and ask them to conform to her. That is not the way the Lord allows life to grow and develop. All are to be in living relationship with the Head, and as that divine life develops, each church emerges differently in features. I would observe again—that among those seven local churches which appeared in the vision John saw there was the same Lord, the same life, the same principle, the same general outlook—and yet, the features characterizing them were very much different one from another. And that is the beauty of life. If everything should become uniform, what would the beauty be in that?

Now in each letter to those seven churches the Lord proclaimed different aspects of himself. Such is what He had revealed of himself differently to each specific church. The Lord is so great that it requires all of the local churches together to come into the fullness of the revelation of Jesus Christ. Let us not assume that we here or we there have all of the revelation. Not so. The Lord is much greater than the church. Let us not think that we individually have contained the Lord, or now have everything, and that there is no more of the Lord to possess. Not so in the least. The Lord is not only much greater than one individual, He is much greater than one local church. It takes all individual saints together to know the length and breadth and depth and height of Christ. Yet, by the same token there is no one local church that can contain all the revelation of God. Even our joint capacity as a church is limited, but He is not.

So we notice here in Revelation 2 and 3 that there is a special revelation of the glorified Son of man given to each of those seven churches. He is found revealing himself to each one of them according to each's various needs and conditions. He did not waste any revelation concerning himself nor did He reveal himself in order for the saints there to store up information about Him in their minds. No, he revealed himself for the purpose of solving their needs as a church. It was most practical in what the Lord did in relation to each local church.

The glorified Son of man is the Christ, the Son of the living God. And since all the saints in all seven of these churches have the same revelation of Him in common with each other as the Lord of all, as the First and Last, as the Living One, and as the All-Victorious One, why would there be any need for different emphases of himself to be revealed, proclaimed and communicated by the Lord to these local churches? It was because of a unique difference in environment within which He had placed the members of each of those churches; and in that particular environment unique to that local church, the Lord's revelation of himself had to be keener and more sharply focused on one particular aspect of himself.

Let us consider, for instance, the church in Smyrna. That was a suffering church, and because it had suffered so much already in that locality, the self-revelation of the Lord to them was more specifically related to the aspect of Him being "the first and the last, the one who has died and who has become alive again." The saints in that local church needed to receive in revelation *that* facet of himself more than any other He could have revealed to the church there in Smyrna. And *that* becomes the testimony of Jesus which was to be communicated and spread in the geographical area of Smyrna.

So there is the same Lord and the same revelation of Him in general, but because of the special environment and circumstances in each church, there will be a special understanding of the Lord and each church will have that special revelatory aspect of Him. And consequently, that special revelation becomes the focus of the testimony concerning Jesus in that specific local church environment. But we can thank God that that does not divide us but unites us, in that in every letter the Lord declared: "He that has an ear let him hear what the Spirit says to [all] the churches." In other words, the letter to one church was to be read by all the other churches. Similarly, there is the instance elsewhere in the New Testament of the apostle Paul's Letter to the Colossians, in which he wrote: "When [this] letter has been read among you, cause that it be read also in the assembly of Laodiceans, and that ye also read that [one] from Laodicea" (Colossians 4:16).

Here we see the greatness of the Lord. Each church has its special feature, its special environment, and accordingly, it is to bear the testimony about Jesus in that special way; and yet, through the fellowship of the churches in the Spirit they may enrich one another and ultimately arrive at "the unity of the faith and of the knowledge of the Son of God" (Ephesians 4:13a). The unity of the Spirit is in the one Lord we have. The unity of the faith and of the knowledge of the Son of God is in that same Spirit. That unity is to be brought in through fellowship. There is to be fellowship not only among individual Christians, there is also to be fellowship from one church to another; and hence, it is by having such fellowship that the churches are increased and united into that understanding of the fullness of Christ. The Lord was therefore looking for himself in those seven local churches. He was looking to see if the application of the special revelation of himself had been realized in each one of those churches in answer to the environment and situation into which that church had been placed by the Lord. If He were to find *that*, then He would be satisfied. If, however, He were unable to observe that realization, then there would be no need for the continuation of the existence of that vessel—of that local church.

What was it that the Lord was looking for in the church at Ephesus? Let us take note that the Ephesian church had many good things: "I know thy works and thy labors and thy endurance and that thou canst not bear evil men and thou hast tried them which say they are apostles and are not and hast found them liars and hast endured for my name's sake and hast not wearied of it." Many good things they had indeed possessed. Nevertheless, what the Lord was looking for in that church was "first love." The Lord therefore granted that church a special revelation of himself in relation to this matter of first love: He reminded the Ephesian saints from whence they had fallen concerning their great love towards Him; for in reading Paul's Letter to the Ephesians one learns that there had been an immense first love in them in the past. How great the Lord loved them, and how much the love of God was in them back then.

There no doubt was life in the Ephesian church, and yet, by the time decades later when the Lord sent this letter of His to that church, the saints there had lost their first love, thus signifying that matters can continue to go on and on and on with all the appearance of goodness in such other things; nevertheless, there is no spiritual life associated with those things due to a lack of first love. And that was what the Lord was looking for in the church at Ephesus as He was walking among those seven lampstands in the Patmos vision. He was not looking for the appearance of goodness among those saints but was hoping and expecting to find a continuance of their first love, which would satisfy His heart afresh. But not finding that precious first love among the Ephesian saints generally, all those other things which were continuing to be done were considered to be empty of any value by the Lord and could not satisfy His heart.

Do we have that first love in us? Do we love the Lord? Do we love Him with a first love—by which is meant the best love? Is that what is behind all our church activities? Are we motivated by this love towards the Lord or do we labor in the church out of a sense of duty or for the sake of appearance? Is the love of God within us? Now that is the testimony of Jesus which the local church at Ephesus had failed to manifest to the world around it. If in our day we love, then the world around us where we are situated will hear of it and see it. They will sense the love of the Lord in us and thus the testimony of Jesus shall be spread abroad.

In the second church, the church in Smyrna, the Lord was looking for "the fellowship of [or, the sharing in] his sufferings" (Philippians 3:10b). Are we suffering with Him and for Him? If we suffer with Him "we shall also reign with him" (II Timothy 2:12). Do we seek a life of ease, of compromise, of comfort? Are we seeking for self-recognition, or are we willing to suffer for His name's sake? If so, then sharing in the Lord's sufferings will be the particular testimony of Jesus which a watching world will receive from us where we may happen to be situated.

Now I sometimes wonder where the testimony of Jesus is. Consider, for instance, the church situation in Red China. Some observers have said that the church has gone underground, and I would agree that that is true. What we can still see *above* ground is not a real church. What some people call the church—the Three-Self Church—is not a real one. Where is the real testimony of the church in Red China? Can it be that the testimony of Jesus is currently hidden underground in suffering? I believe so. His suffering is their testimony.

In the third church, the church in Pergamos, we find that the Lord was looking for a division having been firmly established between the church and the world. For those in this local church, they needed in revelation the facet of the Lord as the one who has a sharp two-edged sword. Here, the Lord Jesus is wielding the same sword mentioned elsewhere in the Bible that divides the soul from the spirit (see Hebrews 4:12b). The church in Pergamos had gotten itself mixed up with the world. In a sense it was now "married" to the world, for the proper noun Pergamos itself means "married." By this mixture having occurred there, there was no longer that sharp dividing and separation from the world which the Lord was looking for in the local church there. Do we in our day have that sharpness of division which distinguishes the church, where we have been planted, from the world? If so, then that is the aspect or facet of the testimony of Jesus for which we are responsible in bearing witness to the world around us.

Now in coming to the fourth church, the church in Thyatira, we find that it is an overwhelming picture. In that overwhelming situation what the Lord was looking for was for the saints in this local church to hold fast to that which is of Him, just as Scripture elsewhere says, "holding fast the head" (Colossians 2:19a). In other words, in the midst of incredible opposition from the enemy within this local church itself, those desirous of being loyal to the Lord were to maintain connection to the Head of the church and hold fast to what they have of Him until He returns. And that would serve to be *their* particular testimony of Jesus locally.

In the fifth local church, the one in Sardis, the Lord was looking for livingness. The believers there were to be living, and not merely having a name of being alive, for though they had a name that they were alive, they actually were dead. So it is a livingness that the Lord was looking for as that which was to be spread abroad of the testimony of Jesus by those faithful saints in this local church.

In the sixth church, the one in Philadelphia, the Lord was looking for His trait of patience. The testimony of Jesus from this local church to the world was for the saints here to reflect in their lives the patience of the Lord, in that they were to be ever persistent in persevering and enduring patiently until the Lord comes again.

In the last church, that in Laodicea, the Lord was looking for His *own* riches in His people. Those in the church had claimed that they were rich. Yes, they were indeed rich in doctrine, but they were woefully poor in spiritual life. The Lord therefore counseled them to "buy of [Him so] that [they] may be truly rich" by receiving "the unsearchable riches of Christ" (Ephesians 3:8b). The Lord was thus looking for believers in this local church who were in possession of His riches and not those of the world. And hence, such would be the testimony of Jesus borne witness to there.

Notice here that the Lord was not looking merely for something good to commend, for those good things do not and cannot explain the reason for our existence as a local expression of the body of Christ. To the contrary, there is but one thing that can determine whether or not the local church of which we are a part should continue to exist or should be phased out, and that is the success or failure of the church in manifesting to the world around it that special feature of the testimony about Jesus which the glorified Son of man had revealed of himself to that church.

Is the testimony of Jesus a reality in us; is it a living matter in us? Have we turned what the Lord has revealed to us into a vital testimony? If so, that is to be the testimony of Jesus which the church of which you and I are members is to spread to the world in the locality where we live and worship.

If the risen, ascended, glorified Son of man can find himself in us—if He can find what He has revealed to us and if it has become our very life—then He is satisfied. No matter what other good things we have, if the life and light are gone, then the glory of the Lord has departed from the church. Even though the Old Testament temple was built with gold and precious stones, once God's glory had departed (cf. Ezekiel 11:23) it was not any different to Him from all the other so-called religious structures for worship.

So let us be focused and concentrate on this one issue: what is the measure of the stature of Christ in us (Ephesians 4:13b)?—what is our testimony as members of a local church in relation to His revelation? Let this be the one matter which truly burdens us. Let this be the one issue in our Christian lives that really concerns us. I believe if we are humble and honest before the Lord, He will grant us the needful mercy and grace.

Chapter Seven

The Man-Child

And a great sign was seen in the heaven: a woman clothed with the sun, and the moon under her feet, and upon her head a crown of twelve stars; and being with child she cried, being in travail, and in pain to bring forth.

And another sign was seen in the heaven: and behold, a great red dragon, having seven heads and ten horns, and on his heads seven diadems; and his tail draws the third part of the stars of the heaven; and he cast them to the earth. And the dragon stood before the woman who was about to bring forth, in order that when she brought forth he might devour her child. And she brought forth a male son [a man-child—AV, ASV], who shall shepherd all the nations with an iron rod; and her child was caught up to God and to his throne. And the woman fled into the wilderness, where she has there a place prepared of God, that they should nourish her there a thousand two hundred and sixty days.

And there was war in the heaven: Michael and his angels went to war with the dragon. And the dragon fought, and his angels; and he prevailed not, nor was their place found any more in the heaven. And the great dragon was cast out, the ancient serpent, he who is called Devil and Satan, he who deceives the whole habitable world, he was cast out into the earth, and his angels were cast out with him.

And I heard a great voice in the heaven saying, Now is come the salvation and the power and the kingdom of our God, and the authority of his Christ; for the accuser of our brethren has been cast out, who accused them before our God day and night: and they have overcome him by reason of the blood of the Lamb, and by reason of the word of their testimony, and have not loved their life even unto death. Therefore be full of delight, ye heavens, and ye that dwell in them. Woe to the earth and to the sea, because the devil has come down to you, having great rage, knowing he has a short time.

Revelation 12:1-12

May I remind ourselves again that the key verse for this series of messages on the book of Revelation is found in verse 10e of chapter 19: "the spirit of prophecy is the testimony of Jesus." God is interested in one thing only: the testimony of Jesus. If He is interested in you it is because of the testimony of Jesus with you. If He is interested in anything else it is because of the relationship it has with the testimony of Jesus. God is interested in this world, for example, because this world is related to that testimony. God is interested in only one thing: the testimony of Jesus.

Now if that is what God is interested in, then it ought to be what we are interested in. I am afraid we have too many interests in competition with God's one interest. Especially do we, who live in this modern world, have too many other interests; and all these crowd in upon our lives to such an extent that we somehow miss the one thing in which we Christians ought to be interested. I would therefore say again that if God

The Man-Child

is interested in solely one thing—the testimony of Jesus—should this not therefore be our one interest on this earth as well? Is there anything more important than the testimony of Jesus? No.

That testimony is today entrusted to His church. We have previously come to understand that the church today is both the vessel for, and instrument of, the testimony of Jesus. This we saw at the beginning of the book of Revelation, for, in its chapter 1 and in verse 1 of chapter 2 we observed in the Patmos vision which John saw that the Lord Jesus was present and walking in the midst of seven golden lampstands. These lampstands, which are seven local churches, were intended to be the reflection as well as the expression of the Son of man who was shown standing in the midst of them. We also learned that these seven churches were measured by one measurement alone: the testimony of Jesus. If they measured up to that testimony, then they would remain in existence. On the other hand, if they did not measure up to the standard of that testimony, they would be removed.

So in our further discussion on Revelation let us bear in mind that the church today is meant to be the depository vessel as well as the instrument for the manifestation of that testimony. And for our time of fellowship today I would like for us to continue to look at the testimony of Jesus in relation to the church at this current age's end-time.

If you have read through the entire book of Revelation, you may have noticed one particular thing. I am afraid, of course, that many Christians have never read this New Testament book. Have you ever read through Revelation at least once? If you have done so not only once but fifty times, then you will have perhaps noticed that after chapter 3 there is no mention of the word church or assembly. It is true that, technically speaking, you do find the word church in Revelation 22:16 where it says, "I Jesus have sent mine angel to testify these things to you in the [churches]." But this mention of the word churches there has nothing to do with this book's chronological order of events. It merely appears there as part of a summary statement of what the Son of man had already done back at the time of chapters 1 to 3 of the book in His having testified to the believers in those seven churches. And hence, one cannot consider this mention of the word church or churches in 22:16 as constituting a fresh and concluding mention of the word in the chronology of events presented in Revelation.

Thus, after chapter 3 we do not find the word church or churches ever appearing again. And because of this absence of the word, some have concluded that this signifies that after the time of Revelation 3 the church has disappeared, having been raptured. Otherwise, they ask, why do we not find the church ever mentioned again in the remainder of the book? They correctly point out that chapter 1 covers those events of "what thou hast seen"; chapters 2 and 3 cover those present events—"the things that are"; and chapter 4 to the end of the book cover those events that constitute "the things that are about to [happen] after these [things]." This, in fact, is how the book of Revelation is to be divided according to Revelation 1:19. Therefore, some say that when the voice came from heaven which said to John: "Come up here," and in obedience he went up in the Spirit, then it was at that moment that the church also went up with John to heaven. The church was raptured to heaven and thus she is no longer on earth; which thus explains, say these Bible observers, why we do not find the word church mentioned again after the book's chapter 3. And hence, these people believe, the church must have been raptured to heaven and is therefore no longer on the earth.

Is this notion correct? It may seem very reasonable to some people since, indeed, the word church is never used again. But I would suggest that even though the word no longer appears after chapter 3, that does not mean that the reality of the church is no longer present in Revelation. Yes, obviously, had the word been used again in the remaining text of the book, the reality of the church's existence on earth could have been more easily discerned; and conversely, because the word has never been employed again, then, of course, it becomes more difficult to find the church after chapter 3; nevertheless, I believe that the reality of the church is still there in the remaining chapters of Revelation.

Before going any further, I need to reiterate what has been said earlier in this series of messages. I do not wish to engage in discussions on different theories regarding the church. I am not concerned with the teaching of whether or not the church will pass through the Great Tribulation. I am not interested in determining whether the church's rapture is to be partial or total in scope or whether it is to occur pre-tribulation or post-tribulation. I am not interested in these matters in and of themselves. You are free to maintain your interpretation and your ideas about these various matters which may be different from mine, for my purpose in these discussions together on the book of Revelation is not to contend or argue about these matters. Rather, my purpose is concerned with only one subject: the testimony of Jesus. This is what we all should be concerned about, since that is this book of Revelation's own acknowledged key for understanding it in its entirety.

So after this hour together has ended you may still maintain your interpretation of things which will have been looked into, and this is quite all right. All I wish to do today is to stress this one point: the testimony of Jesus.

Let me say again that it is quite true that after Revelation chapter 3 the word church or churches no longer makes its appearance, but I believe that an inquiry into several passages which follow chapter 3 of the book will reveal that the reality—if not the name—of the church is nonetheless very much present in the book's remaining chapters.

> And when it [the Lamb] opened the fifth seal, I saw underneath the altar the souls of them that had been

slain for the word of God, and for the testimony which they held; and they cried with a loud voice, saying, How long, O sovereign Ruler, holy and true, dost thou not judge and avenge our blood on them that dwell upon the earth? And there was given to them, to each one a white robe; and it was said to them that they should rest yet a little while, until both their fellow-bondmen and their brethren, who were about to be killed as they, should be fulfilled (6:9-11).

This passage's text is exactly the description one finds in chapter 1 detailing the exile of the apostle John. John had been exiled to Patmos Isle because of the word of God and the testimony of Jesus; similarly, here we learn that these who have been martyred were martyred for the word of God and for the testimony of Jesus. Now it is most certainly clear that those souls underneath the altar, who had been martyred for the word of God and the testimony of Jesus, were Christians. They were undeniably part of the church. Moreover, they were told to wait until more of their fellow bondmen and brethren would be killed—meaning that there will be more persecution to come—that there will yet occur more martyrdom on the earth—and that therefore the total number of the martyrs was yet to be fulfilled.

Now who are going to be those that will be martyred in the future? They will doubtless be those who will have been faithful to the word of God and the testimony of Jesus. Who will these additional martyrs be? Will they not be Christians—believers in Christ? And will they not be part of the church whose membership, when completed, will consist of countless believers in Christ throughout the universe and throughout the ages? Yes, the word church does not appear again, but her reality is nonetheless still there.

After these things I saw, and lo, a great crowd, which no one could number, out of every nation and tribes and peoples and tongues, standing before the throne, and before the Lamb, clothed with white robes, and palm branches in their hands. And they cry with a loud voice, saying, Salvation to our God who sits upon the throne, and to the Lamb. And all the angels stood around the throne, and the elders, and the four living creatures, and fell before the throne upon their faces, and worshipped God, saying, Amen: Blessing, and glory, and wisdom, and thanksgiving, and honour, and power, and strength, to our God, to the ages of ages. Amen (7:9-12).

Here we find an immense numberless crowd assembled out of every nation, tribe, people, and tongue. They stand before the throne and before the Lamb clothed in white robes, with palm leaf branches in their hands, and they lead the angelic host in worship and praise. Who are they? John, who beheld this heavenly scene, did not know; and so, one of the elders, we are told, explained it to Him, as follows:

And one of the elders answered, saying to me, These who are clothed with white robes, who are they, and whence came they? And I said to him, My lord, thou knowest. And he said to me, These are they who come out of the great tribulation, and have washed their robes, and have made them white in the blood of the Lamb. Therefore are they before the throne of God, and serve him day and night in his temple, and he that sits upon the throne shall spread his tabernacle over them. They shall not hunger any more, neither shall they thirst any more, nor shall the sun at all fall on them, nor any burning heat; because the Lamb which is in the midst of the throne shall shepherd them, and shall lead them to fountains of waters of life, and God shall wipe away every tear from their eyes (7:13-17).

Who are they? They come out of every tribe, every nation, every tongue, every people. They are washed in the blood. They have palm branches in their hands. Palm branch in Scripture is a symbol or sign of victory—in this case, a sign of the victory of Christ. They even lead angelic beings in praise and worship. What a position they occupy! And what will be their reward? God will tabernacle over them and they shall serve Him day and night. They shall neither hunger nor thirst and God shall wipe away all the tears from their eyes.

If we turn to Revelation 21:3-4 we shall discover that this is the very description given for the whole church in new Jerusalem.

Yes, I acknowledge again that the word church is no longer used in the text of Revelation subsequent to chapter 3, but no one can assert that the reality of the church is no longer there. On the contrary, her reality is still very much present.

Why, then, is the word church no longer used? If the fact of its absence does not signify the total church's disappearance, then why is it that the Spirit of God chose not to employ that word church or assembly in the remaining chapters of Revelation? I do not pretend to have the definitive answer, but my entire sense on the matter is as follows. Can it be that by the end-time of this present age the church of God will have so departed from the thought of God and will have become so earthly an institution under the dominion of the wicked one that it will appear to be a totally strange and foreign entity to God? That is to say, that because of the utter spiritual declension of the church, it becomes impossible for God to use that word church in reference to many churches so-called lest those who will read the book of Revelation would incorrectly conclude that He considers all of the church to be in a proper spiritual state when that is actually no longer true of her.

The Man-Child

Have you ever noticed that through much usage a word can become so degraded from its original meaning that it eventually takes on an entirely different—perhaps even opposite—meaning?—and that because of that development, people will avoid employing the word anymore lest others draw a wrong conclusion as to what you mean by that term? That, I believe, is what may have occurred with the word church in God's estimation, it having lost its original meaning over time through much careless and inaccurate usage.

And hence, perhaps God at some point felt He could no longer mention church in the unfolding of the rest of Revelation's prophetic narrative lest by His continued use of that term people would incorrectly assume that the spiritual condition of the church in general was in fairly good correspondence with the definition of what God had meant it to be from the very beginning of her existence.

Nevertheless, the above observation concerning the absence of the usage of the word church in the rest of Revelation's text may, in fact, explain a similar instance of a change in terminology used which we can discern in the two letters to Timothy written by the apostle Paul. And let us bear in mind that like the apostle John in his New Testament writings, Paul in his writings was likewise inspired by the Spirit of God to so write.

Let us notice that in the first letter to Timothy Paul is found mentioning "God's house, which is the [church] of the living God" (3:15a); but by the time of II Timothy years later, which was written just before Paul was martyred in Rome, we notice that he did not use the word church in his writing of that letter. Instead, the apostle changes his terminology when referring to the church by writing about "a great house"—here he no longer wishes to say, "God's house." Paul goes on to write, as follows: "in a great house there are vessels of honor as well as vessels of dishonor" (see 2:20); and in the same letter he tells Timothy that whatever he has heard Paul say in the presence of many witnesses he, Timothy, was to entrust to those who were faithful (2:2)—meaning, of course, that there were many others who were unfaithful. Paul also mentions the matter of suffering and persecution and that Timothy should not be afraid to suffer for the testimony of God (1:8b, 2:3, 3:12).

Do we grasp the significance in the change in terminology here? When Paul wrote the first letter he could describe the church as God's house and had no hesitation in using the word church in the further descriptive phrase, the church of the living God; but years later, when writing the second letter to Timothy, he avoided using that word church and only employed the phrase, a great house, in referring to the church, and even abstained from using the term, God's house. Yes, at that time the church was still God's house, but Paul decided, under the inspiration of the Holy Spirit, not to use either that term or the word church. Furthermore, the apostle felt led by the Spirit to issue a call to those who were faithful to be faithful to the very end (cf. 2:11-13).

I believe we can rightly conclude, therefore, that even as early as the time of II Timothy, the church had no longer fulfilled God's intention of what, in His original thought, she was to be and do, and instead, had become something so markedly different negatively that it seems as though, when Paul penned this second letter to Timothy, God by His Spirit was reluctant to move His apostle to call the church His house anymore—let alone, employ the word church.

On the other hand, it may just be that at some point in the end-times there will be such an upheaval and persecution that the real church as such will be totally wiped out leaving not a trace of her existence; but will that mean that the reality of the church will no longer be present? Outwardly the church will seem to have vanished. Though quite pure and quite strong, even so, the true church will probably not be visible any longer to human eyes. Yes, the church of Christianity may still be there, but it will not have measured up to the true character of the real church. The latter, outwardly speaking, will perhaps have been wiped out completely, but the testimony of Jesus will nonetheless continue to go on and on; and could it possibly be that were such a circumstance to occur, might that explain why the word church is no longer mentioned?

I am only suggesting all of the foregoing as possible explanations for why there is the absence of the word church in both Revelation's remaining text and Paul's second letter to Timothy. So please be advised that I am not drawing any definitive conclusions but am simply leaving the matter with you for your consideration.

Now the testimony of Jesus in relation to the end-time is what I wish us to focus upon in today's message; and for this we must go to Revelation chapter 12. There John writes of a great sign which appeared in the heaven: a woman clothed and crowned with various celestial bodies, but she is in travail to bring forth a child and thus she is experiencing birth pangs. However, there appeared another sign in the heaven: an enormous red dragon with seven heads and ten horns, and on his seven heads were seven diadems or crowns; and his tail swept the heaven and flung to the earth one-third of all the stars. Moreover, this great dragon was standing before that woman waiting for the coming forth of the child in order that he might devour the child. But when her child—a male child—comes forth, he is immediately caught up to God and to His throne, and thus the dragon fails in his desire.

And then there is war in heaven: the archangel Michael with his followers fight against Satan and his followers, and Satan and his angels are cast down to the earth and then a voice in heaven is heard saying, "Now is come the salvation and the power and the kingdom of our God and the authority of His Christ; for the accuser of our brethren has been cast out ... : and they have overcome him by reason of the blood of the Lamb, and by reason of the word of their testimony, and have not loved their life even unto death."

Now what is it that God desires us to know from all that? Again let me observe that I am not interested in insisting upon one particular interpretation. There are, of course, many interpretations regarding chapter 12, so many, in fact, that I am reluctant to present you with another one. You may have your own interpretation, and that is perfectly all right. All I am interested in doing today is to provide a spiritual principle which I believe adheres to the testimony of Jesus which, as we have frequently reminded ourselves, is the spirit of all prophecy, including especially this prophetic book of Revelation. I must therefore discipline myself in refraining from giving you another interpretation because the temptation is great to do just that. Even so, whether or not you agree with what I say from this point forward, such is perfectly all right. In fact, I shall remain happy should you end up disagreeing with me. All I ask is that you not argue with me afterwards but that you simply leave the matter there. It can serve as a lesson for us all in that what is more important is that God may truly search our hearts.

Here in this passage we are given to see a woman which, for the sake of discussion, I would suggest that we call her the church. She is clothed with heavenly glory. Is that not the calling and the position of the church? Yes, the church is on earth, and yet her calling and position is in heaven. She is not to be clothed with earthly splendor. For in this present context, if this woman were to be clothed with earthly splendor, we would have to label her as the harlot (cf. Revelation 17). But this woman—the church of God—is not clothed with earthly glory, for oh the church is never to be clothed with that glory. If she is, then she is that other woman. The church is to be clothed with heavenly glory. Indeed, is that not our calling and is that not our position as members of the body of Christ?

The Man-Child

Now this woman is about to bring forth a child and she is currently in travail and is experiencing birth pangs. The woman is in trouble but it is a happy, satisfying trouble, for it is the time for bringing forth a child. When, though, did she begin to conceive? How long back has it been? And does this particular scene bear any spiritual meaning for us?

Let us remind ourselves that for the sake of our fellowship today we have called this woman the church; and the church, as previously mentioned, is to be on earth the depository vessel of, and the instrument for, the manifestation and spread of the testimony of Jesus. But what did we observe in Revelation chapters 2 and 3 concerning this woman? Has this woman—the church—borne a good testimony of Jesus on earth? Or has she, in her seven-fold local expression depicted there, failed in various ways in her mission? We are provided the answer in those two chapters. We learn that all these churches except probably the ones in Philadelphia and Smyrna have failed in bearing a good and satisfying testimony for the Lord. This woman as symbolically portrayed for us in those two chapters has failed, and because this happened, every letter sent out by the Lord to those seven local churches is concluded with a call for overcomers to emerge: he that has an ear let him hear what the Spirit says to the churches; and whoever listens and responds is an overcomer.

Who and what is an overcomer? First of all, let us take note that whoever these overcomers end up being, they are to be found within the church of Jesus Christ. And secondly, there is a need for overcomers because the church in general has failed, thus prompting the Lord to issue the call for those in the churches to respond to Him by taking up the burden for the entire church of spreading the testimony of Jesus to the world around. And thirdly, in answer to an earlier question, the calling of overcomers constituted the beginning of this woman's conception of her child. From this we can perhaps discern that what God intends the whole church to be and do is now to be brought in through the company of overcomers in the church, and that that company—the male child—serves as the prevailing church.

What in essence is a child? And what does that tell us about the parent(s)? In giving answer, let me begin by relating a mother's comment made to me. One day I was called by a sister in the Lord. She stated something quite unusual to me—forgive me for mentioning it—she said she was afraid to see herself in her own childhood by observing the growing-up childhood in her daughter.

Her comment set me to thinking. At times we may not be able to see ourselves very clearly, but if we have a child, that child's upbringing helps us to see ourselves more clearly. How so? It is because a child is the essence of what you or I are. All the special features—the dominant traits of the parents—more likely than not will end up being concentrated and brought out in the children. The children inherit all the dominant characteristics of the parents. They are the essence of the parents and are in fact the continuation of the parents.

Here, then, we are shown in Revelation 12 a woman who has conceived a child. In the light of what has just now been said, what can be said about *this* child and its parent—the church? This child receives in itself the essence of the church. This child also absorbs the concentrated dominant features and characteristics of the church and comes forth as the concentrated continuation of what the church ought to be.

Since the end of the Apostolic Age of the first century this woman, the church, has experienced—whether long term or short term—various kinds of persecution. She had been saved with child, and the day is approaching when there will be even more persecution. The spiritual pressure will be increased; the conflict will be intensified not only outwardly but also inwardly. Even today the church is going through an intensifying period of pressure, and more and more we can hear the groanings of this woman—that is, the groanings of the

The Man-Child

church. More and more in the heart of those who love the Lord there is a groaning within: Oh that the Lord may bring forth what He is after!—Oh that the testimony of Jesus may not suffer!—Oh that there might be some who can be raised up by God to bear the torch!

As time goes on an increasing, intensifying cry of the church can be heard: a crying and an inward groaning. Why? She is in pain; she is in labor, and is about to give birth. Can we hear her cry? And is there not a cry in our own hearts? In those hearts which are towards the Lord there is a cry. I believe we can hear that cry coming forth everywhere throughout the world. The church is about to bring forth her child. She is longing that the child may come forth, because that is her hope and that is her vindication. Thank God that she does not labor in vain. The child shall definitely be brought forth.

But besides the woman in travail there is also another and sinister figure in this chapter 12 scene: the immense dragon. He is standing before the woman, but he seems not to be interested in her. In normal circumstances the dragon, which is God's archenemy Satan (v. 9a), ought to be interested in that woman and concerned about her; but no, he just stands before the woman and waits for her child to be born. In other words, at this moment he is solely interested in the child. Why? Is the child a superman? Not at all. In representation the child is simply the epitome of the normal Christian—one who is being transformed and conformed to the image of Christ (Romans 12:2a, 8:29a). Hence, the child is not a super Christian but merely a normal one who has responded to God.

Let us pause, however, so that we may be clear of one important matter. And that is, that the issue at stake here in this confrontation between woman and dragon—between church and Satan—is not with you or me or with the woman or the child; the issue at stake is the testimony of Jesus. Satan, who is very clever, knows where the central issue lies. He will not in any way be restricted. His whole intent is to destroy the testimony of Jesus because he knows that that will destroy him. Oh, the woman who once had the testimony of Jesus is no longer real. She is of little value to him at this moment but the child is of great value. And why? Because the testimony of Jesus is wrapped up in the child, for the child and not the church is now the real vessel for, and instrument of, the testimony of Jesus at the end-time; and because of this, the wrath of Satan is being poured out upon that child. He intends to devour that child—which is to say, he intends to destroy the testimony of Jesus.

Do we now see the central issue here? The issue today is not with you or me, nor is it with this group or that group. The issue today is not even with Christianity. Satan is too clever for that. The central issue today is where the testimony of Jesus lies. If you are closely related to the testimony of Jesus, the fury of the enemy will come upon you; yet you need not be frightened; for he will not succeed.

The testimony of Jesus is the real issue, and now this issue is to be fought forth over the male child because there lies the testimony. In the end-days of this present Age of Grace God is calling for and gathering in the overcomers and they shall bear the testimony of Jesus on this earth. And again I say, they are not supermen or superwomen. They are not perfect men and perfect women. No, we are told later in chapter 12 that they overcome by reason of the blood of the Lamb. In other words, they had their days of failure, and so, they availed themselves of the precious blood of Christ. They, too, had blemishes, but they have been washed in the blood of the Lamb.

Oh, how much we all need the blood of the Lord Jesus. Overcomers are not people of perfection. No one can ever be one. Nevertheless, in spite of our weaknesses, if we are overcomers, we know the preciousness of the blood of the Lamb. Oh, He cleanses the normal Christian—the overcomer—day by day, moment by moment, so that he or she may be clean and pure.

The Man-Child

Yet more than that, we are told further in chapter 12 that those brethren overcomers overcome the accuser because of *the word* of their testimony. They are not afraid to speak out and bear the testimony of Jesus. They are not afraid to testify that Jesus is Lord. They are not afraid but are willing to lay down their lives if necessary.

Now these are the people whom God is looking for: those who avail themselves of the blood of the Lamb, bear the testimony of Jesus, and love not their lives even to death. Why? Because physical death is nothing compared with spiritual death. Too much is at stake.

How thankful we should be that the Lord is not expecting perfection. He is not expecting supermen and superwomen but ordinary believers who respond to His call. If we should always avail ourselves of the blood of the Lamb that cleanses us, if we are willing to bear the testimony of Jesus and not be afraid to stand for the Lord, if we maintain the attitude that life here and now is nothing to be compared with death unto resurrection and rapture, then by the grace of God we will be counted as overcoming believers in the Age to Come.

Let us be forewarned, however, that because the child is in the womb of the woman, the overcomers cannot and are not to separate themselves from the church, if it is indeed the church; even so, the day is coming when the overcomers shall be separated at the time of the child's birth. Not now, but the day will come, and when that day comes, the child shall be caught up to God and to His throne and Satan will be cast down to the earth; at which moment there comes forth a proclamation: Now is come the salvation and power and kingdom of God and of the authority of Christ.

How and why do all these things happen? For one reason only—the salvation and power and kingdom of God and the sovereign authority of Christ must first become real in the lives of all those overcomers; and because the salvation and power and kingdom of God and the authority of Christ *have* become reality in their lives, therefore, these overcomers are able to cast down the devil and bring in the kingdom.

Do we see the whole picture now? It is most important for us to understand how Satan can be cast out and how the kingdom of God can be brought in. It is only when the reality of the salvation and power and kingdom of God and the authority of Christ is manifested in the lives of the overcomers that there is the spiritual power which can cause the downfall of the enemy.

This we find is the picture of the testimony of Jesus in relation to the church at the end-time. And I do believe we are near the end. True, it is not the end yet, but we are approaching the end. So may God stir our hearts in order that we may respond to what the Spirit of the Lord is saying to the churches.

Chapter Eight

The Man-Child: Firstfruits to God

And I saw, and behold, the Lamb standing upon mount Zion, and with him a hundred and forty-four thousand, having his name and the name of his Father written upon their foreheads. And I heard a voice out of the heaven as a voice of many waters, and as a voice of great thunder. And the voice which I heard was as of harp-singers harping with their harps; and they sing a new song before the throne, and before the four living creatures and the elders. And no one could learn that song save the hundred and forty-four thousand who were bought from the earth. These are they who have not been defiled with women, for they are virgins: these are they who follow the Lamb wheresoever it goes. These have been bought from men as first-fruits to God and to the Lamb: and in their mouths was no lie found; for they are blameless.

Revelation 14:1-5

And I heard as a voice of a great crowd, and as a voice of many waters, and as a voice of strong thunders, saying, Hallelujah, for the Lord our God the Almighty has taken to himself kingly power. Let us rejoice and exult, and give him glory; for the marriage of the Lamb is come, and his wife has made herself ready. And it was given to her that she should be clothed in fine linen, bright and pure; for the fine linen is the righteousnesses of the saints. And he says to me, Write, Blessed are they who are called to the supper of the marriage of the Lamb. And he says to me, These are the true words of God. And I fell before his feet to do him homage. And he says to me, See thou do it not. I am thy fellow-bondman, and the fellow-bondman of thy brethren who have the testimony of Jesus. Do homage to God. For the spirit of prophecy is the testimony of Jesus.

Revelation 19:6-10

And I saw thrones; and they sat upon them, and judgment was given to them; and the souls of those beheaded on account of the testimony of Jesus, and on account of the word of God; and those who had not done homage to the beast nor to his image, and had not received the mark on their forehead and hand; and they lived and reigned with the Christ a thousand years: the rest of the dead did not live till the thousand years had been completed. This is the first resurrection. Blessed and holy he who has part in the first resurrection: over these the second death has no power; but they shall be priests of God and of the Christ, and shall reign with him a thousand years.

Revelation 20:4-6

In our last discussion and fellowship we had begun to move on from considering the testimony of Jesus in relation to His church during the time of the apostle John in connection with Revelation chapters 2 and 3 to a consideration of the same testimony in relation to the end-time as we find it in Revelation chapter 12. We discovered that at the end-days the coming forth of the man-child will be the important development in connection with the testimony of Jesus.

This man-child is actually to be viewed as a body within a body because, symbolically speaking, this child is conceived in the womb of a woman; and if—as I had suggested last time—the woman of chapter 12 represents the church universal, then this man-child is a collective entity representing the company of overcomers. It is thus a body within a body, but this man-child inner body is that which comes out of the church-universal outer body. They are not separated; they are together. But the day will come, at the end-time of this present age, when this man-child shall be brought forth in birth, and at that time this much smaller body of the man-child shall be separated from the larger body, the universal church. And when that separation-event occurs, it shall be the end of this current Age of Grace.

It was indicated last time that God is calling for overcomers *within* the church. You and I as believers in Christ cannot be separated from the church. We *can* be separated from a building; we *can* be separated from an organization; we *can* be separated from an institution or from a religious system; but we can *never* be separated from the church of God because it is a living organism. We who now belong to Christ have been born into it and have therefore become a part of it. And we each can become an overcomer, but an overcomer still remains in, and part of, the church. Accordingly, all overcomers as the man-child constitute a body within a body. But the day is coming when that man-child shall be brought forth in birth, and instantly upon *that* happening, he is caught up to God and His throne, to be followed immediately thereafter by a series of other events which shall occur.

As we learned from chapter 12 last time, there will be the breakout of war in heaven: Michael and his holy angels will fight against Satan and his fallen angels. And consequently, there will no longer be any place in heaven for Satan, that is, no place for him in the clouds anymore; for Satan, along with his fallen angels, will be flung down upon the earth. Now what can you expect if Satan comes to the earth? You can expect nothing but a period of great tribulation. There will be great trouble on this earth as never before seen because now Satan will be personally stationed *on earth*—and no longer in the clouds—with all his hosts of evil forces. For there is then heard a great voice from heaven saying, among other things, this: "... the accuser of our brethren has been cast out, ... Woe to the earth and to the sea, because the devil has come down to you, having great rage, knowing he has a short time" (12:10c, 12b).

We are given to understand from Revelation chapters 2 and 3 that the call for overcomers is issued to individuals: "He that has an ear let him hear what the spirit says to the churches." We must hear and respond individually. Nevertheless, though the call goes out to individuals and the response must be made individually, the testimony is corporate in nature. In other words, it is not that one is called to bear the testimony all by himself or herself; rather, all those who have responded to the Lord individually will at the end-time bear the testimony of Jesus together.

In Christianity today, especially among the fundamentalists, we hear that the number of those to be saved must be fulfilled; and when the number of saved ones is fulfilled, then Christ will return. Have you heard this? Well, that is a very true statement, for there is scriptural basis for this assertion. In Romans 11, for example, we read: "... until the fulness [full number] of the [gentile] nations be come in: and so all Israel shall be saved" (see vv. 25b-26a). Hence, there is a definite number of all those who shall be saved and brought into the flock or church of God. And when that number is fulfilled, Christ shall return. This understanding is very true, but we do not know what the sum of that completed number is to be. We only know that the number must and will be reached before Christ shall return. This is absolutely a true understanding.

The Man-Child: Firstfruits to God

Yet, let us also be aware that it is equally true that the man-child—as a collective entity—must be completed as well before Christ shall return. Is God one who is only after quantity? Is He not one who is likewise interested in quality? What if God should see realized and completed the full number of the redeemed and yet all those saved ones turn out to be so poor in spiritual quality that they can neither endure the time of testing nor bear the testimony of Jesus? What, then, is the use of such a quantity? I am not implying here that God does not wish the number of saved ones to be reached—He does so wish; I am only wanting to point out that what God emphasizes equally as much, and more, is the quality and not just the quantity. The quantity of saved souls may be there but if the spiritual quality is absent in them, then the total result may as well be discarded since they are of no use or value in fulfilling the purpose of God. But if God has quantity *and* quality, then He is satisfied.

In order that the number of those who are to be saved can be realized we *must*, of course, preach the gospel. Yes, indeed, there is the necessity and the urgency in preaching the gospel of Jesus Christ to all the world. As we are definitely instructed in Scripture, the gospel must first "be preached to all the nations, and then the end shall come" (see Matthew 24:14). How true that is! I do feel the burden of preaching the gospel and I do feel the burden of reaching every soul possible. Oh do let us bring the unbelievers into the kingdom and into the body of Christ that they too may be saved. This is very important. Oh that we may have more burden, and be more on fire, for the gospel and that we may have more compassion for lost souls. Oh that we may be used by the Lord to bring many unsaved people into the church—into the body of Christ! The number of the saved must indeed be fulfilled! Let us be more responsible in gathering them in. Even as Jesus was desirous of teaching this through one of His kingdom parables, let us go out into the highways and invite them to come in to the wedding feast of the king's son and fill the wedding hall (Matthew 22:2, 9-10).

This is what we all must certainly do. But let us not forget that in this same kingdom parable of Matthew 22, when the king came into the banqueting house to see his guests, he noticed that one of them was not dressed in a wedding garment, and so he ordered that the guest be cast out. Thus signifying that if guests were not clothed with wedding garments, they must be cast outside into the darkness where they shall regret not having been properly dressed.

Yes, on the one hand, we must preach the gospel and bring many souls to Christ; on the other hand, we must realize that God is looking for quality. He will not be satisfied with mere quantity and little or no quality. He will not tolerate that. God's people must measure up to His standard, for He is constantly looking for quality. "Man looketh upon the outward appearance," says Scripture, and that, among other things, has reference to quantity and number; "but," this passage of Scripture continues, "Jehovah looketh upon the heart" (I Samuel 16:7), and that speaks of quality and spiritual value.

We find such spiritual value in the man-child, as revealed in Revelation 12. There *is* a number for the man-child, but it is the number of quality and not that of quantity. When the man-child shall be completed—that is to say, when those who respond to the Lord's call for overcomers have satisfied God's heart—then the Lord Jesus shall return.

In all the past centuries many have given their very lives for the testimony of Jesus. Let us notice that when the fifth seal spoken of in Revelation 6:9-11 is opened, we are given to see under the altar those who had already been martyred for the word of God and for the testimony of Jesus they had maintained. There were many of them, but their number was not yet complete; for the word to them was for them to wait until the number of their fellow servants and brethren who were to be killed for the testimony of Jesus, as they had been, was completed.

We understand from this, therefore, that the number of overcomers collectively making up the man-child must likewise be fulfilled. There are many throughout the generations and centuries who have stood faithfully and suffered for the testimony of Jesus, but their number will not be complete without many others entering into the same suffering and bearing the same testimony. Consequently, what the glorified Son of man is looking for today is the completion of the man-child. What He is looking for today is the completion of the spiritual value of the testimony of Jesus.

At this point in our discussion today I would put forward this question: Do you have any problem when reading what Ephesians 4:13-14a says?—"until we all arrive at the unity of the faith and of the knowledge of the Son of God, at the full-grown man, at the measure of the stature of the fulness of the Christ; in order that we may be no longer babes, tossed and carried about by every wind of that teaching ..."? In reading these verses, do you have a problem? I do. When can this state of spiritual maturity ever be reached? The more I study church history, and the better understanding I have of what is happening in Christianity today, and the more I ponder the future, the less I am confident that that goal is possible.

Christianity is more divided than ever before. Instead of a "unity of the faith and of the knowledge of the Son of God," we find there are far, far more differences and divisions now as compared to what existed by the close of the first century of the church. Christians today are seemingly all divided. This Scripture passage speaks of that desired spiritual maturity of the church as being like "a full grown man"; currently, however, it seems as if the church is dwindling down to becoming more like a collection of carnal babes! This passage also speaks of the desired goal for the church as finally measuring up to the stature of Christ's fullness. Where concerning the body of Christ as a whole today do we see anything like that being manifested? Not much, if at all! So if it is true—and it is—that Christ's return must wait until His body is fully grown, then I do not know how much longer He must wait. He has already waited a full twenty centuries. Must He wait another twenty centuries?

I inquire again, Does Ephesian 4 at all trouble you? How can the measure of the stature of the fullness of Christ in the body be realized? How can that goal of the Lord be achieved? Can such a tremendous outcome be fulfilled in our generation? Does it currently look even in the least like that? I must acknowledge here that these verses and the questions arising from them have troubled me considerably over the years.

According to Ephesians 5 Christ's body must be perfected before it can be presented to Him as His bride; but I ask you, Where is the perfection of the body appearing in our day? From what we can observe today, it seems that the church is receding further and further away from this desired goal. Indeed, instead of that maturing standard growing higher in the church, it would appear to be going in the other direction—lower and lower. Now how can this problem be solved? What, if He has one, is God's answer and solution to this difficult problem?

I remember once talking with our brother Watchman Nee about this when we were together. He had a possible answer. Yes, he noted, the body must be matured; there must be full growth; there must be the full stature of Christ evident in the body of Christ. But how can it be attained? I recall brother Nee stating that he felt that this is to be attained through the overcomers: that when the overcomers have come to a completion, that is when the man-child is completed: And when the man-child has been completed, then God considers that the whole body of Christ has been completed.

Now if this be the case, how important it is for the man-child to be completed! How important it is, therefore, for you and me to respond to the Lord's call to be overcomers! On the other hand, if we remain as the *overcome* instead of rising up as overcomers, it will not only be a personal loss, it will also be a loss to Christ and His church. What, then, is the hope of the church? That hope is dependent upon those who refuse to be the overcome but desire to be overcomers.

This very desired outcome can rightly be likened to the Biblical principle of the firstfruits of the field which we find typified in Revelation 14:4c and in Old Testament typology. We know—according to the Old Testament and according to common agricultural knowledge—that when a crop of grain is planted in a field, there will later be, but before the harvest time, the ripening of the firstfruits. Back in Old Testament times the farmers would therefore cut the firstfruits first, they having already ripened before the rest of the crop. And because those firstfruits ripen early, they are always the best in quality and taste. Now after cutting the firstfruits, the farmers were required by Jewish law to present them to the priest; which is to say, that these firstfruits were to be presented to God as an offering acceptable to Him. And after having presented the firstfruits of the grain crop the farmers waited for the rest of the field to ripen, and then came the general harvest.

This common farming knowledge was closely adhered to in the old economy and priestly law of the Jewish nation. And spiritually, this principle is applicable to us believers today. God has sown His redemptive seed in the field of the world. He has been waiting patiently for His harvest time to arrive, but let us remind ourselves that before God's general spiritual harvest can be realized there must first be the ripening and cutting of the firstfruits. Spiritually speaking, therefore, if the general harvest represents the gathering in of the whole believing church unto Christ himself, then what does the ripening and cutting of the firstfruits represent? That represents the gathering in of all the overcomers in the church.

As indicated a few moments ago, this term firstfruits is used in Revelation 14:4 and has to do there with the 144,000 on Mount Zion. I am not going to explain the 144,000 in a dogmatic way. There are some sects in Christianity which assert that this number of 144,000 has already been reached and even claim that their members themselves comprise those 144,000. Well, I am not interested in those assertions and claims, nor am I going to argue with them as to whether or not they constitute the 144,000. God knows; and furthermore, we do not need to know. But here in this prophetic vision of Revelation 14 we learn that there are 144,000 standing on Zion. And this Scripture passage further informs us of this: "These have been bought [or, purchased] from [among] men [and offered] as firstfruits to God and to the Lamb" (v. 4c).

We see here the firstfruits all right; but perhaps you will ask: But where is the harvest? Well, further on in this same passage, beginning at verse 14, we are told what John also saw:

> And I saw, and behold, a white cloud, and on the cloud one sitting like the Son of man, having upon his head a golden crown, and in his hand a sharp sickle. And another angel came out of the temple, crying with a loud voice to him that sat on the cloud, Send thy sickle and reap; for the hour of reaping is come, for the harvest of the earth is dried. And he that sat on the cloud put his sickle on the earth, and the earth was reaped.

What have we found here? We have initially found the firstfruits of heaven—standing, we are told, on Mount Zion. I believe this 144,000 on Mount Zion are not the same as the 144,000 mentioned in Revelation chapter 7. Some say that these 144,000 on Zion are the same group, but if we read the relevant passages carefully, we will realize that they are not. The first mention of 144,000, in chapter 7, refers to the number of those who have been sealed from among the twelve tribes of Israel; but the 144,000 here in chapter 14 are not those who are sealed. The first group of 144,000 from among all twelve tribes of Israel are sealed in order for them to be kept or preserved through the Great Tribulation alluded to in 7:1-3; but this

The Man-Child: Firstfruits to God

second group of 144,000 are on Mount Zion, that is, they are located above the earth—in other words, in heaven. The 144,000 in chapter 7 have their foreheads stamped or sealed with the name of the living God; but here in chapter 14 we are told that those in this group of 144,000 are sealed on their foreheads with the name of the Father and of Christ the Lamb. Now this latter group cannot have reference to Israel but must have reference to those in the church—and not even have reference to the whole church but only to those who at that time make up the church triumphant. In other words, what is being referred to here is the firstfruits of the church. They have become ripe before the general crop harvest has ripened.

For the sake of clarity, let us inquire as to how a sheaf of wheat or corn gets ripened. Well, the sun will shine upon it, scorch it, and dry it up until it is fully ripened. And once it is ripened the root will be so loosened from the soil of the earth that you can merely touch it and it will come out.

With all of the aforesaid as background, let us apply all this to ourselves today. We believers in Christ are still currently out in the crop field, which is the general harvest that is yet to occur. We are to be ripened as the days go by via suffering, persecution for the name of Christ, a denying of ourselves and taking up the cross, and experiencing the discipline of the Holy Spirit—all such, if responded to positively, will ripen us. These circumstances and spiritual experiences will loosen us from the soil of the earth: from the world. In fact, we are told in Luke 21 to be watchful lest the cares and pleasures of this world (vv. 34-35) will so hold us down to the earth that when the Lord commences His return appearing, we will not be ready to ascend—that is, to be raptured as those who have overcome.

Does it really matter if we live a life under the discipline of the Holy Spirit or else live a life in the flesh? After all, are we not saved and will we not therefore go to heaven? What difference does it make anyway? Allow me to say that there is a great difference, a *very* great difference. Let us understand the time factor here, for it is important. Those who are counted among the firstfruits ripen first. How do they become ripe first? Under the scorching of the sun—that is to say, under the discipline of the Spirit of God—they become dried up as far as the earth is concerned. They are so lost to this world that a mere touch will rapture them to heaven.

Is that not wonderful? On the other hand, if the Lord should come today and call us up, would He find a thousand tons of weight attached to us? Are we so tied to the earth that it would be like tons of weight holding us down? Those, though, who have overcome the world have cast off whatever weights which would have hindered their spiritual progress in the Lord (cf. Hebrews 12:1a), and thus they will qualify to be among the firstfruits that have ripened first. And being firstfruits, they are the best and can be presented and offered up to God; and they shall be priests to Him and to Christ the Lamb (Revelation 20:6c).

Let us now take a closer look at these 144,000. With our current focus we need not be interested in whether or not the 144,000 is a literal number. It can be, nothing is impossible with God. It may instead be a figurative or symbolic number, since 144,000 is the result of the multiplication of 12 x 12,000. In the Bible we find that 12 is a perfect number. It represents the completeness of completeness. We do not know, nor do we need to know, exactly what this signifies in this context. Either way, we have before us a company of people. Whether this number 144,000 represents only one elite company from among the overcomers or whether it is symbolic of all the overcomers—we do not know. We only know for certain that this 144,000 are the firstfruits offered up to God and to His Christ. Let us read again the opening verse of Revelation 14: "And I saw, and behold, the Lamb standing upon mount Zion, and with him a hundred and forty-four thousand."

Let us next recall what the writer of Hebrews tells us in chapter 12: "ye have not come to [Mount Sinai] ..., but ye have come to mount Zion; and to the city of the living God, heavenly Jerusalem" (vv. 18a, 22a). Is not the heavenly Jerusalem our goal? Is not our goal Mount Zion? Here in Revelation 14 we learn that these people have reached the goal. They have possessed the prize of their high calling. They have so pressed on in Christ that they have arrived at Mount Zion. Are you pressing on as we all are encouraged to do in one of the apostle Paul's letters?—"... forgetting the things which are behind ..., I press on toward the goal unto the prize of the high calling of God in Christ Jesus" (Philippians 3:13b-14 ASV).

Are you pressing on? What is the condition of your spirit? Is it the spirit of going forward, or is it the spirit of sitting back in ease and comfort? If those 144,000 have reached the goal, they have arrived on Mount Zion because they had pressed onward and not held themselves back.

If you desire to press onward and upward, you cannot live a life of ease, comfort and pleasure. You have to overcome all obstacles. You must allow yourself to come under discipline. You must run the race of your Christian life as if you are the only one able to gain the prize (I Corinthians 9:24-25a). This is what is involved in reaching Mount Zion. These 144,000 had reached that heavenly summit. Thank God for that!

> And I heard a voice out of the heaven as a voice of many waters, and as a voice of great thunder. And the voice which I heard was as of harp-singers harping with their harps; and they sing a new song before the throne, and before the four living creatures and the elders. And no one could learn that song save the hundred and forty-four thousand who were bought from the earth.

And consequently, these 144,000 sing a new song. The new song is the song of redemption found in Revelation 5. The old song is the song of creation found in Revelation 4. They were purchased by the blood of Christ. They have experienced the redemption of the Lord in such a way that they can sing a song that no one else can. No one else can sing it because it has to be learned by experience.

Furthermore, it is as though these overcomers are playing harps. The harp is a musical instrument of the heart. In playing the harp a person must literally embrace it and touch its strings as though touching one's own heart. And the song which emerges comes from the player's heart. Thus, these are people who have experienced the redemption of the Lord in such a way that they have a new, heartfelt song to sing.

May I inquire, How much do you know and have experienced of the redemption of Jesus Christ? Do you only know that you have been redeemed out of death into life, or do you know that you have also been redeemed from the bondage of the law and all which that means? How much do you actually know of Christ's redemption? These folk sing a new song from their hearts' experience of the Lord Jesus in His redemptive love.

Concerning these overcomers, we are also told in Revelation 14 that "these are they who have not been defiled with women, for they are virgins." In Matthew 25 we read of the Lord's parable of the ten virgins. Spiritually speaking, all believers are virgins, for our relationship with Christ is that of a virgin to her Lord. In position and in name all believers are virgins. But some virgins have been defiled and some have not. Some are virgins in name but their hearts are not pure towards Christ. Their Christian lives have been compromised and thus they have been defiled. But there are those who are not only virgins in name but also in actuality. Their hearts are pure towards their Lord and their lives are not compromised. And such are those wise virgins mentioned in Matthew 25. They shall have part in the Bridegroom's marriage feast, but those foolish virgins mentioned in Matthew 25 will be shut out. Let not any of us say or think that the foolish virgins are unbelievers. Unbelievers are not virgins at all. These foolish ones are virgins and yet they have been defiled.

Another description of these 144,000 which is given to us in Revelation 14 reveals that "these are they who follow the Lamb wheresoever it goes." They are not followers of man but followers of the Lamb. Yes, we ought to give respect to those who should be respected; but we must follow the Lamb and follow Him wherever He goes. Let us not follow the Lamb where He goes only when and where it is convenient for us, but let us follow Him wherever He goes. If He goes to the cross, we also must go there. If He goes to the throne, if He enters glory, we also follow. Let us follow the Lamb wheresoever He goes.

Now these various descriptions and qualities are of those who are the overcomers! If there is no other qualification required of an overcomer, I think this last one would be enough. If we should forget everything else about the overcomers, let us simply remember this one quality of theirs: they follow the Lamb wheresoever He goes, and that is sufficient. Are you following the Lamb in this manner?

There is one final description given of these 144,000: "and in their mouths was no lie found; for they are blameless." They dared to be true. These overcomers were not afraid to speak forth the word of the testimony of Jesus, for they were blameless. In this connection, we read in Ephesians 1 that believers "should be holy and blameless before him in love" (v. 4b). Overcomers are those who are blameless, yet not because they have no fault, but they are blameless because they desire to please the Lord. They are blameless in love.

Such will be the company of the overcomers that will constitute the firstfruits offered to God. These are they who shall bring in the downfall of Satan from the clouds of heaven to the earth. These are they who shall bring in the kingdom of God. These are they who shall attend the marriage feast of the Lamb. These are they who shall be the armies that are clothed in white and following the Lamb in that final victory. And these are they who shall sit on the throne and be kings and priests and reign with Christ for a thousand years.

The overcomers are needed urgently. They are so important because they will be used by God to bring in the future kingdom age. And in that Age to Come they shall reign with Christ for a thousand years. Praise God!

Chapter Nine

The Kingdom and New Jerusalem

And I saw a new heaven and a new earth; for the first heaven and the first earth had passed away, and the sea exists no more. And I saw the holy city, new Jerusalem, coming down out of the heaven from God, prepared as a bride adorned for her husband.

Revelation 21:1-2

And he carried me away in the Spirit, and set me on a great and high mountain, and shewed me the holy city, Jerusalem, coming down out of the heaven from God, having the glory of God. Her shining was like a most precious stone, as a crystal-like jasper stone; having a great and high wall; having twelve gates, and at the gates twelve angels, and names inscribed, which are those of the twelve tribes of the sons of Israel. On the east three gates; and on the north three gates; and on the south three gates; and on the west three gates. And the wall of the city had twelve foundations, and on them twelve names of the twelve apostles of the Lamb. And he that spoke with me had a golden reed as a measure, that he might measure the city, and its gates, and its wall. And the city lies four-square, and its length is as much as the breadth. And he measured the city with the reed—twelve thousand stadia: the length and the breadth and height of it are equal. And he measured its wall, a hundred and forty-four cubits, a man's measure, that is, the angel's.

Revelation 21:10-17

And I saw no temple in it; for the Lord God Almighty is its temple, and the Lamb. And the city has no need of the sun nor of the moon, that they should shine for it; for the glory of God has enlightened it, and the lamp thereof is the Lamb. And the nations shall walk by its light; and the kings of the earth bring their glory to it. And its gates shall not be shut at all by day, for night shall not be there. And they shall bring the glory and the honour of the nations to it. And nothing common, nor that maketh an abomination and a lie, shall at all enter into it; but those only who are written in the book of life of the Lamb. And he shewed me a river of water of life, bright as crystal, going out of the throne of God and of the Lamb. In the midst of its street, and of the river, on this side and on that side, the tree of life, producing twelve fruits, in each month yielding its fruit; and the leaves of the tree for healing of the nations. And no curse shall be any more; and the throne of God and of the Lamb shall be in it; and his servants shall serve him, and they shall see his face; and his name is on their foreheads. And night shall not be any more, and no need of a lamp, and light of the sun; for the Lord God shall shine upon them, and they shall reign to the ages of ages.

Revelation 21:22-22:5

The key to the entire series of discussions we have thus far engaged in together on the prophetic book of Revelation, and which we shall continue to engage in as the Lord leads, is that fragment found in verse 10 of this book's chapter 19: "the spirit of prophecy is the testimony of Jesus." I am deeply concerned with the testimony of Jesus, and I believe we all should likewise be concerned because this is God's chief interest. God is not interested in anyone and any thing other than the person of His Son and the testimony of His Son—the Lord Jesus. And because of that, we are only interested in past and present history if such is related to the testimony of Jesus. And we are likewise only interested in future history, which is prophecy, if, again, it is related to the testimony of Jesus.

It was mentioned previously that the testimony of Jesus has been entrusted to the church today, and in our past times of fellowship together on Revelation we have briefly traced this matter of the testimony of Jesus from the beginning of the church at Pentecost, following Jesus' resurrection/ascension, to the end-times and even to the age which is to come after that. We must now go forward further, but before doing so I would like to mention just this much, which is, that the testimony of Jesus is not only to be maintained during this present church age but is also to be maintained even in the Age to Come. And what is meant by the term Age to Come is Christ's kingdom age. In the kingdom which is to come the testimony of Jesus is to be maintained by those overcomers who are the firstfruits offered to God and to the Lamb.

We are quite familiar with the Lord's prayer so-called. Actually, that is the *church's* prayer, because that is what Jesus had taught the church to pray. Now we are all familiar with those words within that prayer which say, "let thy kingdom come, let thy will be done, on earth as it is in heaven" (see Matthew 6:10). Today we are very much aware that the kingdoms of this world are not yet the kingdom of our God and of His Christ (cf. Revelation 11:15b). We know, of course, that the word of God currently prevails in heaven but it is often being opposed on earth. So our prayer today is still: Thy kingdom come: May all the kingdoms of this world become the one kingdom of God and of His Christ. Today, also, our desire is that God's will may be done on earth as it is in heaven—that His will may prevail on earth—that there shall be no opposition nor hindrance but that His will shall prevail on this earth as it is in heaven.

And we realize that this prayer which Jesus had given to His church must be answered, and it is going to be answered. The day is approaching when the kingdom of God shall be established upon this earth. The time is coming when heaven shall rule over this earth and that is to be the time—the age—of the millennium, a thousand years of the kingdom age. It shall be the time when heaven rules over the whole earth.

Let us inquire as to how, during the coming kingdom, the testimony of Jesus will be maintained. Or may I put it this way: In the kingdom age the testimony of Jesus is to be the governing principle that reigns over the entire earth; but how is the sovereign reign of the testimony of Jesus to be maintained? I believe it is to be maintained by those who have overcome. Because they have suffered with Christ today, therefore, they shall reign with Him tomorrow. Because this earth has witnessed their much suffering while they spent their days of humiliation on this earth, so, in like manner, this same earth shall be witness to their glorification: they shall reign with Christ for a thousand years.

When people believe in the Lord Jesus, there is more involved than simply going to heaven. Yes, indeed, heaven is our future home; for we will go to heaven and be with Christ forever and ever. That is immensely good and precious, but there is more than heaven for those who have been faithful followers of the Lamb. There will come a day when those who have been faithful, when those who have gladly received the testimony of Jesus and have borne that testimony well and who have even paid with their lives for it, shall be rewarded; for they shall reign with Christ for a thousand years over this same earth where they had once suffered so much. It is a most comforting thought, and it is most fitting that the place where they suffered shall be the very place where they shall be glorified.

The Bible tells us that the overcomers shall shepherd the nations with an iron rod. As a matter of fact, this phrase appears three times in the book of Revelation.

> (1) And he that overcomes, and he that keeps unto the end my works, to him will I give authority over the nations, and he shall shepherd them with an iron rod; as vessels of pottery are they broken in pieces, as I also have received from my Father (2:26-27).

In this first appearance, it is the promise made to the overcomers in the church at Thyatira. It is promised to the overcomers that they shall shepherd the nations with a rod made of iron. When will they shepherd the nations? Today they are persecuted and hostilely pursued by the nations; but there will come a day that the nations shall be shepherded by the overcomers whose symbol of authority and rule shall be like that of an iron rod. But when? It will begin at the arrival of the Age to Come.

> (2) And she brought forth a male son, who shall shepherd all the nations with an iron rod; and her child was caught up to God and to his throne (12:5).

Here it is said concerning the man-child that he shall shepherd all nations as though utilizing a rod of iron in doing so.

And finally (3) this same phrase appears a third time, but in this instance it is said in reference to Christ:

> And out of his mouth goes a sharp two-edged sword, that with it he might smite the nations; and he shall shepherd them with an iron rod; and he treads the wine-press of the fury of the wrath of God the Almighty (19:15).

Here in this last instance this special phrase is used in speaking of Christ. He is to shepherd the nations with an iron rod. The scene of his rejection and the scene of his humiliation shall be the very location where he shall rule with an iron rod.

Notice, however, that in the preceding two Scripture passages this special description has reference to the overcomers in the church. Those who overcome and are not overcome by the world shall one day shepherd the nations in a way as though using an iron rod. Just as Christ shall shepherd the nations, so shall they also do; for what will be true of Christ shall likewise be true of them. The overcomers shall reign with Christ for a thousand years, and in the process they—like *the* Overcomer—shall shepherd the nations with a rod of iron.

Now when we hear the word shepherd, what is our immediate impression? Does it not cause us to think instantly of tenderness—of tender care, unlimited patience, sacrificial love, boundless compassion? That is what being a shepherd of sheep reminds us of. If you are a shepherd, you must be tender towards them because if you are not tender but very rough and rude, your sheep will ultimately be beaten to death. A shepherd must also have limitless patience. Sheep, as we know, can be very foolish animals; consequently, a shepherd must exude sacrificial love, to the point of even laying down his life for his sheep. There must be boundless compassion in a shepherd as well: if his sheep go astray, then he must have unlimited compassion in going forth to find them and bringing them back to safety. That very word shepherd gives us the impression of such love as that.

But here in all three of these passages we are told that Christ and His fellow overcomers shall shepherd all the nations *with an iron rod.* Now with what kind of impression does a rod made of iron provide us? Does not that phrase, an iron rod, instantly remind us of strength and toughness? In the Thyatira passage, in fact, the glorified Son of man describes what shepherding the nations with an iron rod will be like: "As vessels of pottery are they broken in pieces." Thus, this descriptive phrase, with an iron rod, expresses the notion of authority that, being supreme and full of strength, will not tolerate any opposition or hindrance of any kind to its rule.

How can anyone reconcile or put these two opposite impressions together? For do not these two phrases—"a shepherd" and "iron rod" give off two opposite impressions? Indeed, have you or I ever seen a shepherd shepherding his sheep with an iron rod? Never in this world. Yet, the day is coming when the glorified Son of man and His fellow overcomers shall shepherd all the nations with an iron rod. In other words, during the coming kingdom age of a thousand years the heavens shall rule in such a way that both tender love and supreme authority shall be united and manifested together. Contrary to the coming age of Christ's kingdom, if today we love, we usually forfeit authority; and if today we exercise authority, we normally forfeit love. But the time is soon coming when there shall be the unhindered expression of love that is united perfectly with the unhindered exercise of authority.

Why is it that these overcomers of the church are qualified to rule with Christ for a thousand years? Again, let me remind ourselves of what the purpose for their rule is: it is for the purpose of establishing and maintaining the testimony of Jesus. During the kingdom age the testimony of Jesus shall remain the supreme principle governing all nations. Any challenge or opposition to that governing principle shall swiftly be put down with supreme authority and with sovereign power as shall be exercised by both *the* Overcomer and His fellow overcomers, for these overcomers are qualified to rule in the future because today the testimony of Jesus has been wrought into their very constitution. To explain it another way, Jesus' fellow overcomers represent the testimony of Jesus themselves because they have the testimony of Jesus in themselves. Because they have suffered for the testimony of Jesus and because they have established that testimony in their own lives, therefore, they are eminently qualified to establish and to maintain that same testimony throughout all the nations during their thousand-years co-reign with Christ.

Hence, let us adopt for ourselves that heavenly motivation and keep it ever before us. It can serve as a holy incentive for us to press on and qualify to be co-rulers with Christ in the coming kingdom age. The days of affliction here below are temporary; nevertheless, those days of righteous suffering and affliction shall work a glorious reward for us eternally; so let us not be discouraged but let us be renewed in strength by the Spirit, and let us resolve to press on continually till the day of the Lord's return appearing.

Let us understand, however, that the ushering in and duration of the kingdom will not be the final consummation of the ages. For after the thousand years the old earth and old heaven shall be consumed with fire (II Peter 3:10, 12b). There shall be no more place for the old heaven and earth but there shall be a new heaven and a new earth, and then New Jerusalem shall descend out of heaven upon that new earth, after which Eternity—the Ages of Ages—shall be ushered in, with the testimony of Jesus prevailing and manifesting its fullest expression by means of New Jerusalem, called also, the holy city.

So during our remaining time today I would like for us to consider together the testimony of Jesus in relation to the coming age of eternity. Let us therefore not assume that the expression of the testimony of Jesus is only for our present age. Inasmuch as the Lord Jesus is eternal, so His testimony is eternal as well. No matter how strong the testimony of Jesus may be on this earth currently it is nonetheless weak; no matter how full it may be today, it is nonetheless only partially so. Hence, we do thank God that in the coming Eternity the testimony of Jesus shall be manifested in full strength with no end to it, as will be seen in the holy city of New Jerusalem. It is quite true that there shall be a new heaven and a new earth, but the center of attraction will be New Jerusalem.

What is this New Jerusalem? What do people imagine the holy city to be like when contemplating the description of it which Revelation chapters 21 and 22 provide? Well, some have pointed out that it can be likened to a giant lampstand. We will recall that at the beginning of Revelation the Lord had shown to His apostle John in the book's first vision seven golden lampstands, which we learned represented seven selected churches from among all those then in existence in the Roman province of Asia. Thus, that first vision showed us the local church; namely, the local church of God in Ephesus, the local church of God in Smyrna, the local church of God in Thyatira, the local church of God in Pergamos, the local church of God in Sardis, the local church of God in Philadelphia, the local church of God in Laodicea, and by extension, the local church of God in New York, the local church of God in this place and that place throughout the world. That was what was shown John in representation in that first vision of Revelation. These seven lampstands were, each of them, to be the vessel in which the testimony of Jesus was to be deposited and through which the testimony was to be expressed to the world around. In other words, the testimony of Jesus was to be deposited and maintained in the church locally everywhere on the earth. But by the conclusion of Revelation's entire prophetic narrative we find that all these local expressions of the church for manifesting the testimony of Jesus shall be merged into one.

The Key to "Revelation"

For in this book's final two chapters we do not see *seven* golden lampstands or any multiple of sevens but we see only one holy city that some have likened in shape to that of one gigantic lampstand. Let us therefore take a close look at several of its many features having especially to do with the shape of a lampstand—one gigantic one, indeed!

An angel said to John, "Come, and let me show you the holy city, New Jerusalem, the bride of the Lamb" (see Revelation 21:9b-10). So John was led in the Spirit and saw that city from atop a great and high mountain. I believe that speaks of spiritual elevation which enabled the apostle to see every part of New Jerusalem. For example, he saw its twelve foundations. Today, we do not normally see the foundation of a building, for it is hidden underground; but in the case of New Jerusalem, the day is coming when its many foundations shall be as visible as its superstructure.

This city is built entirely differently from our architectural concept. There is no time for me to interpret concerning these twelve foundations, made of twelve different precious stones; and in any case, may the Lord restrain me from giving an interpretation. This I *can* say, however, that these twelve foundations are not so arranged that all are laid out horizontally side by side but are most likely situated vertically one atop the other. Which means that there is an immense height involved with just the *foundation* of New Jerusalem! Try, if you can, to picture in your mind's eye those twelve foundations one upon the other, and all consisting of twelve different precious stones. Oh, how massive, how brilliant, how multi-colored it all is! These combined foundations ascend up and up and up. And that is but the *base* of this one gigantic lampstand; nevertheless, what a beautiful base it is!

And then there is the wall which, when measured by the angel, is 144 cubits high by man's measurement, which was what the angel was using. That, incidentally, is another beautiful aspect to the holy city, New Jerusalem: a man's measurement is different from that of an angel; but the day is coming when a man's measurement is an angel's, and vice versa, because men shall be like angels—spiritual angels—as the Lord Jesus once said (Revelation 21:17b, cf. Matthew 22:30). And thus that high wall serves as the trunk of the one giant lampstand that is New Jerusalem. No longer do we see seven branches here but a single stand alone because the one lampstand that is the holy city, New Jerusalem, speaks of the unity which is in Christ.

And next we can visualize that upon that immensely high stand there is its lamp, which, we are told, is the Lamb. This important detail we earlier read from chapter 21 verse 23: "the glory of God has enlightened it, and the lamp thereof is the Lamb." Because a lamp needs its lampstand, therefore, we can rightly conclude that, symbolically speaking, the holy city can be visualized as one gigantic lampstand with the Lamb being a part of it. And as we just now read, the light by which to enlighten the holy city is the glory of God. Hence, what we see pictured here is one beautiful, giant lampstand.

By looking more closely at this immense lampstand that is the holy city of Revelation 21-22, we may perhaps be reminded of that much earlier lampstand of Exodus 25 which God had commanded Moses to make for the tabernacle. I believe many have been fascinated by its description. Just recently a brother telephoned me to explain in some detail the cups and their shape which are mentioned in the Exodus passage as being part of that lampstand. Whether I agree with him or not, that is another matter. That is a matter of interpretation which we need not go into here. Nevertheless, that brother was most fascinated by just the shape of the cups of the lampstand made by Moses for God's tabernacle in the wilderness and which later was placed in Jerusalem's holy temple. Cups, flowers, buds, and so forth have been the objects of fascination for many when contemplating Moses' beautiful golden lampstand in tabernacle and temple of old. Much more beautiful and fascinating is this giant lampstand which is now pictured so gloriously for us here in Revelation.

Just the materials alone which make up certain elements of *this* lampstand are fascinating enough. There are precious stones such as jasper and transparent gold, and there are pearls so large that just one of them constitutes but one gate—and it is not a small gate, either. There is nothing to be seen here of hay nor wood nor stubble (cf. I Corinthians 3:12). Everything is made of gold, precious stones, or pearls. Oh, what incomparable materials there are here! Moreover, let us take note that all these materials have one very special quality unique to them alone: all are perfectly pure, a quality not to be found on earth today. Have you ever seen a piece of gold that is perfectly transparent? You will not find such on earth. Even glass, though it may be said to be transparent, is nonetheless impure to one degree or another; for when light is beamed through the glass, it holds back or hides some of the light. In the case of this giant lampstand that is the holy city, New Jerusalem, all materials constituting it—whether gold, pearl, or precious stones of every kind—all are of such fine and pure quality that they are perfectly transparent.

With respect to the golden lampstand in the Jewish temple of old, the light which emanated from the seven branch-lamps and that thus shone upon the stand or candlestick of the lampstand, caused the light to be reflected, and by this means the light was multiplied and increased. But what do we see happening here in the holy city of New Jerusalem? As has been noted earlier, New Jerusalem is itself, symbolically speaking, one tall gigantic lampstand. And but one lamp is atop it—the Lamb of God himself—and God's glory is enlightening and enveloping the entire city with the light of the one lamp. And because everything in the city is perfectly transparent, there is total undistorted reflection of the light throughout the city. And hence, the light of God's glory is so reflected everywhere that

His glory fills the city with overflowing light which in no way is ever diminished but instead is magnified continually.

Here on earth, no matter how good the quality of gold is, it is at best perhaps 98% or 99% gold; and if it is 95%, that gold is considered pure already, but it is still not 100% pure gold. On earth, everything is alloyed, adulterated, a mixture. Despite every effort to purify gold and other precious metals, there cannot be 100% purity. Is this not a picture of man at his unsuccessful best in his attempt at purifying himself? The day is coming, however, when we who are the Lord's shall reflect Christ in such a way that there is no shame, no taint or shadow of sin, no need of hiding as did the first man; instead, we shall be perfectly transparent—instead, we shall be so pure that the testimony of Jesus can pass through a people in undiminishing light, and all "the nations shall walk by that light" (cf. Revelation 21:24a).

Today, we Christians ought to be the light of this world (Matthew 5:14a). And as we have just now seen, according to Revelation 21:24a the nations shall ultimately walk in the Christians' light. But in contrast to that future glorious situation there are many in Christianity today who are walking in the light—which actually is the darkness—of the nations. Too many believers today are imitating and copying the world. Many—perhaps among us, too—are following the world: in fashion, in custom, in habit, and even in moral standards. In almost every respect much of the church is following the world now; and hence, no wonder that the church has plunged into spiritual darkness. Oh, may we who claim to be followers of Christ truly be the light of the world—yet, not because *we* are the light but because Christ is the light and because, if true of us, His testimony is with us and in us and is being spread through us to the world.

I pray that the work of purification is taking place day after day in our lives. We must be purified of the dross and impurities of all that is of ourselves, and all that is of Christ must be wrought and incorporated into us; and if day by day by day this work of purifying and transforming is taking place in us, then the day will come, thank God, when there shall be none of self but all shall be of Christ. He must truly be all and in all; for He is truly the First and the Last, He is truly the All-Inclusive One; and because He is the All-Inclusive One in us and among us, therefore, all shall be transparent with no shade or shadow whatsoever. And hence, further, if Christ is magnified in us and with us and is not distorted, diminished, or hindered in any way, our reflection of Him shall be perfect.

Is that not the cry of those who love the Lord today? Oh that we may be transparently pure; oh that we may be all of Christ and none of ourselves. Should that not be our cry, that Christ may be reflected in us in a perfect way and not distorted? Is it not to our shame that when people look at us they do not see in us the Christ as He truly is? If so, no wonder He is disgraced in us because we have misrepresented Him. How we hold back His glory, how we distort His testimony, how we bring shame to Him. Is that not a crime? If we have His life, oh that we may be transparently pure so that the testimony of Jesus may truly be full and rich.

Truly, we must live with Eternity in mind. Let us not live for the here and now. Yes, we must live today and not be concerned about the next day because one day's trouble is sufficient for that day (Matthew 6:34b); instead, we must constantly live with Eternity in view, and if we so live that way we shall desire to be pure and transparent in order that we may be like Him even as He is (I John 3:2-3).

In view of all which has been said here, the first and foremost impression I would like for us to have in relation to the holy city as a giant lampstand is that we may all desire to have the testimony of Jesus be formed and manifested fully and richly in and through us to the world without any shadow or shame and that all the nations shall be able to walk in the light of God's glory as reflected in and through us as the holy city. If so, the nations shall no longer stumble and fall because they now walk by the light of God's glory as reflected in the holy city; and their rulers, consequently, shall voluntarily bring their splendor and glory into New Jerusalem (Revelation 21:24, 26).

Permit me again to say that I am not interested in interpreting various portions of Revelation but I am merely wishing to relate what to me is a very important spiritual principle for us to weigh and consider. Having said that, let me proceed by asking this question: What in actuality does this holy city represent or symbolize? Well, you might say that the holy city represents the church. What church? Oh, the universal church; and in support of your answer, you might say that in Revelation chapters 1, 2 and 3 we see the church local, and now in Revelation chapters 21 and 22 we see the church universal. And you would be correct in asserting all that.

But may I ask one other question? How universal is your universality? It is quite true that the holy city has twelve foundations bearing the names of the twelve apostles of the Lamb who in their persons represent all those who have been, and shall yet be, saved during the current New Testament era. In other words, you would also be correct in saying that from this Biblical fact we can conclude that all who are redeemed by the precious blood—from the very first to the very last person, from the greatest to the smallest—everyone is included there because the twelve names of the twelve apostles of Christ are there: none is lost; and we can also conclude that all such believers in Christ shall reach what Paul has described as the maturity of a spiritually full-grown person and the entire measure of the fullness of the stature of Christ (Ephesians 4:13b). Such is the marvelous working of God. All those who belong to God in Christ are there and none of them is lost; for the Lord Jesus said that no one can take anyone away from Him nor from His Father (John 10:28-29).

But I would ask you again, How universal is your universality when speaking of the church universal? Does not the holy city include more than those saved during the New Testament era? For do we not also read in this same passage of Revelation that there are twelve gates with the names of the twelve tribes of Israel inscribed thereon? Surely the names of the twelve tribes of Israel represent together all the saints who lived and died during the Old Testament era: therefore, Abraham, too, will be there in the holy city, Isaac likewise will be there, also Jacob; we most certainly will meet David and Jeremiah there as well. All the saints from the Old Testament period shall be found among New Jerusalem's residents. Even with that, however, does all the foregoing constitute the extent of your universality?

Let us consider further what this passage in Revelation 21 additionally indicates. Are there not twelve angels who are stationed at the aforementioned twelve gates? Even the good angelic beings are well represented as being in the holy city. In other words, we see in New Jerusalem the consummation or the ultimate gathering up together of all the grace and glory of God from the very beginning to the very end. All is consummated together in providing a final everlasting testimony to the name of Jesus. Let us recall again the words of chapter 12 of Hebrews: We do not come to Mount Sinai but to Mount Zion—to the city of the living God which is the heavenly Jerusalem, to myriads of angels in joyful assembly together (the universal gathering), to the church of the firstborn whose names are registered in heaven, to God the judge of all, to the spirits of righteous men made perfect, to Jesus the mediator of a new covenant, and to the sprinkled blood that speaks a better word than the blood of Abel (vv. 18, 22-24).

In these words of Hebrews 12 and in the description of the holy city in Revelation 21 we find the consummation—the ultimate, final gathering up—of all the work of God throughout the centuries and ages which touch not only the earth but also heaven, and touch not only men but also angels. Indeed, we learn that everything shall be gathered up together in order to give a final and permanent witness to all concerning the testimony of Jesus.

Let us briefly review once more what has been said previously concerning what the testimony of Jesus essentially is. Please recall those few verses in Revelation chapter 1 which record what the glorified Son of man said to His apostle: "I am the first and the last, I am the living one who was dead and am alive forever and ever, and I hold the keys to death and hades" (see vv. 17c-18). So what is the testimony of Jesus? It is a witness to the fact that (a) He is the First and the Last—the All-Inclusive One who shall be all and in all; (b) He is the Living One—the One full of resurrection life; and (c) He is the All-Victorious One—for He has the keys to death and Hades.

Now if *that* is the testimony of Jesus, what do we see in the holy city? Do we not see there the very same thing displayed in all its fullness and glory? Does not the entirety of New Jerusalem bespeak a testimony testifying that Christ is surely the First and the Last?—that He is all and in all who fills everything in every way?—that everything speaks of Him? Everything in the holy city does speak of Christ in all His purity and transparency. All in the holy city betokens Christ and nothing else. We also find there the river of the water of life and the tree of life—indications, are they not, that everything in New Jerusalem is full of the divine life. And finally, we find there as well the throne of God and of the Lamb—the all-victorious Christ.

Such is the testimony of Jesus, and this testimony shall be fully and richly maintained throughout Eternity—the Ages of Ages—to the praise of the glory of God.

TITLES AVAILABLE
from Christian Fellowship Publishers

By Watchman Nee

Aids to "Revelation"	The Life That Wins
Amazing Grace	The Lord My Portion
Back to the Cross	The Messenger of the Cross
A Balanced Christian Life	The Ministry of God's Word
The Better Covenant	My Spiritual Journey
The Body of Christ: A Reality	The Mystery of Creation
The Character of God's Workman	Powerful According to God
Christ the Sum of All Spiritual Things	Practical Issues of This Life
The Church and the Work – 3 Vols	The Prayer Ministry of the Church
The Church in the Eternal Purpose of God	The Release of the Spirit
"Come, Lord Jesus"	Revive Thy Work
The Communion of the Holy Spirit	The Salvation of the Soul
The Finest of the Wheat – Vol. 1	The Secret of Christian Living
The Finest of the Wheat – Vol. 2	Serve in Spirit
From Faith to Faith	The Spirit of Judgment
From Glory to Glory	The Spirit of the Gospel
Full of Grace and Truth – Vol. 1	The Spirit of Wisdom and Revelation
Full of Grace and Truth – Vol. 2	Spiritual Authority
Gleanings in the Fields of Boaz	Spiritual Discernment
The Glory of His Life	Spiritual Exercise
God's Plan and the Overcomers	Spiritual Knowledge
God's Work	The Spiritual Man
Gospel Dialogue	Spiritual Reality or Obsession
Grace for Grace	Take Heed
Heart-to-Heart Talks	The Testimony of God
Interpreting Matthew	Whom Shall I Send?
Journeying towards the Spiritual	The Word of the Cross
The King and the Kingdom of Heaven	Worship God
The Latent Power of the Soul	Ye Search the Scriptures
Let Us Pray	

The Basic Lesson Series
Vol. 1 - A Living Sacrifice
Vol. 2 - The Good Confession
Vol. 3 - Assembling Together
Vol. 4 - Not I, But Christ
Vol. 5 - Do All to the Glory of God
Vol. 6 - Love One Another

ORDER FROM: 11515 Allecingie Parkway Richmond, VA 23235
www.c-f-p.com

TITLES AVAILABLE
from Christian Fellowship Publishers

By Stephen Kaung

"But We See Jesus"
—*the Life of the Lord Jesus*
Discipled to Christ
—*As Seen in the Life of Simon Peter*
In the Footsteps of Christ
God's Purpose for the Family
The Gymnasium of Christ
The Key to "Revelation" —Volume I
New Covenant Living & Ministry
Now We See the Church
—*the Life of the Church, the Body of Christ*
Shepherding
The Songs of Degrees
—*Meditations on Fifteen Psalms*
The Splendor of His Ways
—*Seeing the Lord's End in Job*

The "God Has Spoken" Series
Seeing Christ in the Old Testament, Part One
Seeing Christ in the Old Testament, Part Two
Seeing Christ in the New Testament

ORDER FROM: 11515 Allecingie Parkway Richmond, VA 23235
www.c-f-p.com